The Hamlyn
KNITTING
GUIDE

The Hamlyn

KNITTING
GUIDE

Rae Compton

Hamlyn
London · New York · Sydney · Toronto

The publishers would like to thank Mr and Mrs H.
Firmin for allowing photographs to be taken in their
home.

Photography by Michael Plomer
Line drawings by Jill Shipley

First published in 1980 by
The Hamlyn Publishing Group Limited
London · New York · Sydney · Toronto
Astronaut House, Feltham, Middlesex, England.

Filmset in England by Photocomp Ltd., Birmingham
in 9 on 10pt. Univers Medium

Printed in Hong Kong
ISBN 0 600 30501 5

Contents

Chapter 1

Preparation

Throughout many hundreds of years man has used natural fibres to create fabrics with a knitted appearance, even though the method of working these often differed radically from that used today. No longer have knitters to spin and dye the yarn they use, instead they can choose the type and texture of yarn they want from a wide range.

Few other crafts require so little basic equipment or so small an initial expense for such a rewarding result. Furthermore, knitters can choose to work from detailed stitch-by-stitch instructions, they can adapt existing patterns to incorporate distinctive ideas or, with endless stitch variety, they can create entirely their own designs.

The method of placing the loops on the needles, knitting and purling the stitches and casting off the work is easily learnt and requires only a pair of needles and a ball of yarn.

Use a pair of 4 mm needles for learning and a ball of double knitting wool. It is important to practice with wool as this has a greater resilience than man-made fibres and is easier to use. Yarn that has been used before or was bought because it was a bargain should be put aside until the stitch formation and patterns are familiar. There will be plenty of time later to use up oddments.

Needles

Needles are made in several different lengths as well as in a range of different thicknesses and are sold in pairs for flat knitting or sets of double-pointed needles for round knitting. There are also circular needles (see page 107). Altogether there are 17 different thicknesses of needle ranging from 2 mm, for very fine lace work, to 10 mm, which are used for chunky yarns and which make the work grow in length very quickly. Needles are made in lengths of 25, 30 and 35 cm and it may well depend on which part of the country you come from as to the length you prefer. Knitters in the southern counties tend to use the shorter lengths while in the north, particularly in Scotland, the longer lengths are used as this allows one needle to be tucked under the arm to keep it in place and so gives extra support and increases the speed with which the fingers can move.

Needles can be bought as they are required until a selection of sizes has been acquired but it is useful to keep them in a needle case where they can be found easily and they do not become unnecessarily bent or scratched.

Cable needles

These are short needles used to hold slip stitches while others are worked and are made in one or two sizes only. It is not necessary to have them in the same size as that being used for knitting as the stitches are never left on them for any length of time; it is best to use one finer than the needles in use so that the stitches are not stretched as they are moved. Cable needles can also be useful in dealing with stitch transfers and picking up dropped stitches and should be part of your equipment.

Work container

A work bag or box is not essential but it is useful to have some sort of container to keep work tidy and to hold the other items that will be needed. These are as follows:—

Ruler	Tape measure
(*metric and imperial*)	(*metric and imperial*)
Wool needles	Scissors
Pins	Row counter
Stitch holder	Cable needles

Always make use of both a flexible tape and a rigid ruler. The tape is required for taking measurements round a person or item but other measurements, both of work in progress or finished sections of knitting, must always be made on a flat surface and a more exact measurement will be obtained with a rigid rule. At all times avoid measuring with the work on your knee or on a padded chair arm.

Wool needles

Special needles with a large eye and a blunt tip are available at drapers and wool shops for sewing up garments. The advantage of using these, rather than ordinary sharp-tipped needles, is immense, for the blunt end slips between stitches rather than through the strands of yarn and leaves neater, tidier seams.

Scissors

A small, sharp-tipped pair of scissors will come in useful for unpicking a seam that is not perfect and is essential for cutting man-made yarns which cannot be broken. Keep the ends from doing damage by sticking them into a cork.

Pins

Dressmakers' steel pins, which are rust resistant, are less likely to cause staining of the yarn, particularly when used during making up, either in blocking the garment, when both damp and heat may be present, or in pinning together sections which are not sewn together immediately.

Row counters

The easiest way of saving time is to work always with a row counter. In this way a routine can be established and when working a pattern there will be no doubt in your mind which row you are knitting. A row counter which slips onto the end of the needle is easily seen but one which incorporates a dial and can be used for the counting of patterns worked, numbers of increases worked or the required number of decreases needed widens the scope of help given and can save you having doubts as to the point you have reached, even after the knitting has been left aside for some time.

Stitch holders

Stitches which are being held apart from the main work may be slipped onto safety pins but are much better held on stitch holders designed for this purpose. Small and large holders are available and both are a necessary part of your equipment.

Yarn

Yarn is the name given to any fibre suitable for knitting. The most usual division is into natural and man-made yarns.

Natural yarns

These can be divided into two groups: those obtained from plants and including cotton and linen, and those made from hair, wool or fur from animals. The latter includes wool from sheep, hair from goats and fur from rabbits.

Natural yarns still have many qualities which are less easily supplied by man-made fibres but they are becoming increasingly expensive.

Man-made yarns

Made entirely from chemicals, man-made yarns are hard-wearing and easily laundered although they may lack something of the warmth and elasticity associated with wool. They include nylon, Courtelle and Acrylic fibres. Experiment into the quality of these fibres is continual and each year the yarns available for hand knitting have more of the qualities of natural yarn.

Mixed yarns

To make the best of both types of yarn, many mixtures of wool and man-made fibre are used and these retain the best qualities of both.

Buying yarn

All the yarn needed for one garment should be bought at the same time to ensure that it comes from the same dye lot. Each batch of yarn dyed is stamped with a specially allocated number on the ball band. Yarn from another batch is likely to vary, if only very slightly, but this is often sufficient to cause a noticeable line of colour difference across a garment.

Fig. 1

Chapter 2

Making a start

Knitted fabric is made in two ways, either by knitting in rows, which is called flat knitting or knitting in rounds, which is called round knitting or circular knitting.

Fig. 2

Flat knitting

Flat knitting is worked on two needles and the piece of knitting gradually lengthens as each row of loops is made out of the previous row. Garments made in this way are worked in sections and seamed together or 'made up', when the sections are all completed.

Round knitting

Round knitting has the advantage of producing seamless garments and is worked on sets of four, or more, needles with points at both ends or on a circular needle. Although beginners tend to start with flat knitting, round knitting is no more difficult and should not be overlooked or left untried. Some techniques, such as those used in producing Fairisle and Norwegian-patterned garments are more easily made in rounds where all the rows of pattern are facing the knitter, and the gradual formation of the coloured design can be seen at a glance.

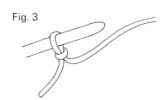
Fig. 3

Casting on

Whichever type of knitting is used, the making of the first row of loops from which the knitting will grow is called casting on. There are many different ways of casting on, each with its own advantage and use, but there are only three methods that need to be learnt right from the start.

A fourth method, which produces a much better finish and should be used on all visible ribbed edges is explained on page 120 and is shown on the striped knee socks and the lace-patterned V-necked sweater. It can be used as soon as

Fig. 4

Fig. 5

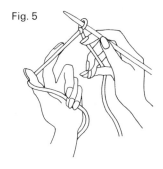

knitting and purling have been practised and is worth the extra time that it takes.

The three most used methods of casting on are

1 The thumb method, which makes a strong, elastic edge and can be used for all casting on except lace.
2 The two-needle method, used for lace and for all stitches that are cast on at side edges after the work is in progress.
3 The cable method, also used for every cast on except lace, and gives a strong reliable edge.

Making a slip knot

Any cast on begins with a slip knot which is used as the first stitch. It is made by folding the yarn over itself in a circle (fig. 1), drawing a loop through this circle (fig. 2), and placing the new loop on the needle, drawn up to the needle so that it is neither slack nor tight (fig. 3).

The thumb method

This method uses one ball of yarn and one needle. To practise it make a slip knot about 30 cm from the yarn end and place it on the needle, holding the needle in the right hand. Wind the yarn round the right-hand fingers by placing it round the little finger, over the next finger, under the middle finger, finishing with it over the forefinger, which is used to guide it round the tip of the right needle as the stitches are worked (fig. 4).

Smooth, regular knitting is a result of controlling the flow of yarn to the knitting and this is achieved by wrapping the yarn round the fingers instead of allowing it to hang loose. However odd it may feel it is essential at this point to become used to picking up the yarn round the fingers so that a habit is formed. The order of wrapping may be altered provided that the yarn finishes over the forefinger held above the right needle. The forefinger can then move forward and round the needle tip without moving the rest of the hand off the needle.

Place the needle in the right hand, between thumb and finger like a pencil and loop the short end of the yarn across the front and round the back of the end of the thumb, holding the end lightly against the palm with the last two fingers (fig. 5).

*Insert the needle tip under the thumb loop (fig. 6) and using the forefinger loop the yarn attached to the ball under the tip of the right needle and over the top from left to right, beside the thumb loop already picked up (fig. 7).

Draw the tip of the needle through from back to front under the thumb loop (fig. 8), placing the

Fig. 6

Fig. 7

right forefinger behind the stitch on the needle so that it will not slip. Gently draw the short end until the slack has been removed (fig. 9).

Rewind yarn round thumb and fingers and draw another loop through, repeating from * until the required number of stitches have been cast on.

The length of yarn required before the slip knot varies with the number of stitches to be cast on. A rough guide is to allow three times the length of the cast on edge. Surplus length can always be used for making up and is better than leaving too little and having to rework the edge completely.

The two-needle method

This uses one ball of yarn and two needles. Make a slip knot about 10 cm from the yarn end and put it onto one needle. Place the needle holding the loop in the left hand and take the other needle in the right hand, after winding the yarn round the fingers as given for the thumb method.

* Insert the right needle tip through the loop from front to back under the left needle. Take the yarn under the right needle tip to the left then back to the right up over the needle, close to the loop on the needle (fig. 10).

Draw the tip of the right needle through the loop from back to front so that there is one loop on each needle (fig. 11).

Slip the new loop onto the left needle and draw it up (fig. 12). Cast on other stitches in the same way working from the *.

The two-needle cable method

The first and second stitches are worked in the same way as just described for the two-needle method.

To work the next and succeeding stitches place the right needle between the two stitches on the left needle nearest the tip. Bring the yarn round the needle tip and draw a loop through in the same way, placing it on the left needle (fig. 13).

To knit stitches

Take the needle with the stitches in the left hand and the other needle in the right, with the yarn wound round the right fingers.

* Insert the tip of the right needle from front to back through the first stitch, under the left needle (fig. 14).

Using the right forefinger bring the yarn under the right needle tip and up over the top of the needle towards the right (fig. 15). Draw the loop on the right needle to the front through the loop on the left needle (fig. 16).

Slip the left needle out of the stitch, leaving the

Fig. 8

Fig. 9

Fig. 10

Fig. 11

Fig. 12

new loop on the right needle (fig. 17). Repeat from the * until each stitch on the left needle has been knitted.

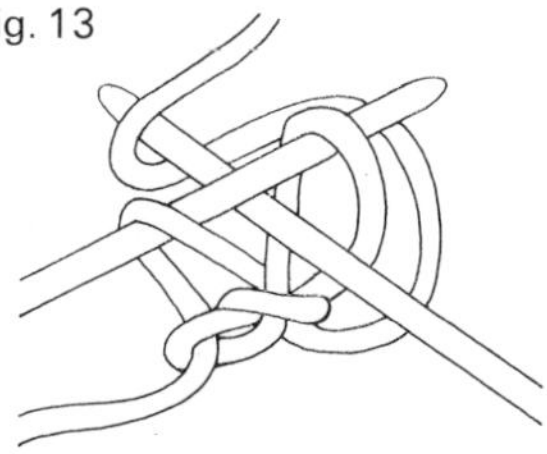

The next row is worked in the same way, after changing the needles so that the stitches are in the left hand and the free needle in the right. When every row is knitted the ridged pattern that the stitches make is called garter stitch.

To purl stitches

A knit stitch gives a smooth surface to the front of the stitch and forms a ridge behind the stitch. A purl stitch is the reverse, forming a ridge across the front of the stitch and leaving the back smooth.

* To purl a stitch insert the right needle tip through the stitch on the left needle from the back towards the front, with the right needle in front of the left (fig. 18), and the yarn at the front.

Fig. 13

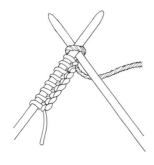

With the yarn over the right forefinger take it over to the left ending under the right needle tip (fig. 19). Draw the loop on the right needle through the left loop towards the back (fig. 20). Slip the left needle out of the loop so that the new stitch is on the right needle. Repeat from the * until a purl stitch has been worked into each cast on stitch.

Casting off

Casting off is worked when a knitted section is the required length and is a means of securing all the stitches so that they do not slip out of the last row to be worked.

Fig. 14

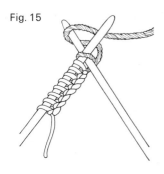

Knit the first two stitches. Using the tip of the left needle lift the first stitch over the second and right off the needle tip (fig. 21).

Knit the next stitch so that there are two stitches again on the right needle. Lift the first over the second and off the needle; continue in this way until only one stitch remains. Cut the yarn leaving an end not less than 10 cm, and draw the end through the last stitch.

Fig. 15

Purl stitches are cast off in the same way except that they are purled instead of knitted. Where both knitted and purled stitches are used on the last row they should be worked as they were with knitted stitches being knitted and purled stitches being purled, always lifting the first over the second as they are worked onto the right needle.

Joining yarn

The joining of yarn when one ball is finished and a new ball is required should be done as invisibly as possible and is best kept at the side edge. Leave an end of yarn from the finished ball, at least 10 cm long, at the row end. Leaving a similar end, loop the new yarn over the needle and continue to work the row. When the knitting is completed the ends can be darned into the side seam.

To prevent the ends of thick yarn unravelling, lightly knot the two ends together while the work is in progress, then unpick the knots and work the doubled ends into the knitting. Never leave knots.

Fig. 16

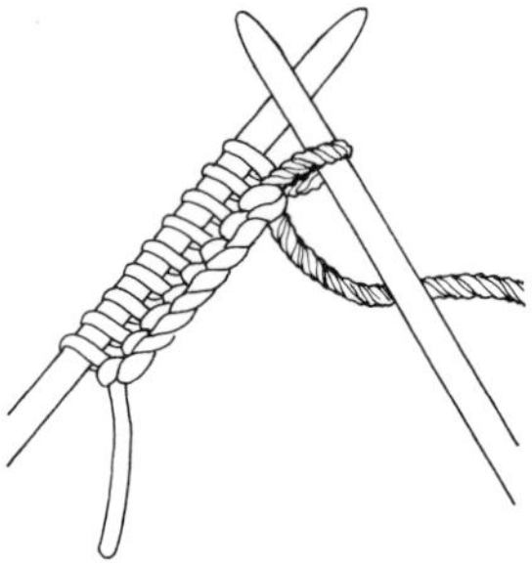

Project: Long or short waistcoat

Fig. 17

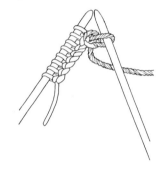

Straight sections worked in garter stitch make a waistcoat in a long or short version, which makes a welcome addition to any wardrobe and provides practice in casting on and off.

Materials
The yarn used is Patons Husky 11 (12: 14) 50 g balls for long version.
8(9: 10) 50 g balls for short version.
1 pair 6 mm needles.

Measurements
To fit an 85(90: 95) cm bust, 34 (36: 38) in.
Long version, length from shoulder 67.5 (67.5: 72.5) cm.
Short version, length from shoulder 45 (45: 47.5) cm.

Tension
7 stitches and 14 rows to 5 cm measured over garter stitch worked on 6 mm needles.

Fig. 18

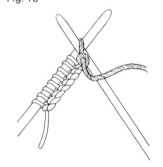

Back
Using 6 mm needles cast on 62 (66: 72) stitches, using the thumb or cable method.
Work in garter stitch (every row knit) until back measures 50(50: 52.5) for long version or 27.5(27.5: 30) cm for short version.
Cast off.

Left front
Using 6 mm needles cast on 31(33: 35) stitches.
Work until same length as Back.
Cast off.

Right front
Work as given for Left Front.

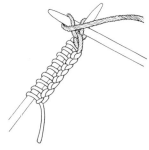

Fig. 19

Back yoke

Using 6 mm needles cast on 26(28: 30) stitches
for armhole edge.
Work in garter stitch until yoke is 10 cm less
than cast off edge of Back, approximately
35(37.5: 40) cm.
Cast off.

Right front yoke

Using 6 mm needles cast on 26(28: 30)
stitches to make the armhole edge.
Work in garter stitch until strip measures
approximately 10(11.25: 12.5) cm.
Shape neck
Cast off 12(13: 14) stitches at beginning of
next row, knit to end. Work 7.5 cm on these
remaining 14(15: 16) stitches.
Cast off.

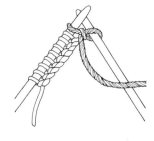

Fig. 20

Left front yoke

Work as given for right front yoke, working one
row more before casting off 12(13: 14)
stitches for neck shaping.

To make up

Seam back yoke to cast off back edge
overlapping the cast off edge on the right side
of the yoke to form a ridge and leaving 5 cm
each side to form the underneath of the
armhole. Sew the front yokes to the fronts in
the same way.
Seam the front shoulders to the back.
Join side seams of back and fronts to yoke.
To make ties
Using 6 mm needles cast on 46 stitches. Cast
off.
Work a second tie in the same way and sew to
either side of the yoke.

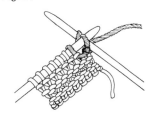

Fig. 21

Chapter 3

Simple Patterning

Knit and purl stitches present a different appearance and are the only ways of working stitches apart from leaving a stitch unworked. It is from the difference between the two appearances and the variations in combinations of the two stitch types that all pattern grows.

Knit stitches

Stitches that are knitted have a smooth front with the stitch loop forming a small V shape and across the back is a horizontal loop.

Purl stitches

The purl stitch is the reverse of this having a horizontal loop across the front and a smooth V-shaped back.

Garter stitch

Garter stitch consists of a row of smooth V shapes followed on the next row by another smooth row but because the work has been turned the ridge or horizontal loop shows on the right side above the smooth shape (fig 22). Although it is usual to work garter stitch by knitting every row it is also possible to achieve the same effect by purling every row but in this case the work is not usually quite so regular.

  Because garter stitch has an equal number of smooth loops and horizontal loops on either side of the work it lies flat even before pressing and, in fact, seldom needs to be pressed to look its best. This makes it useful for edgings and double-sided fabrics.

continued on page 21

Fig. 22

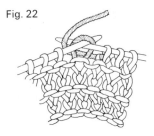

Opposite *Long version of Waistcoat, the ideal project for a beginner (pattern on p. 14).* Overleaf *Left Zipper Jacket with cable motif (pattern on p. 84). Right Norwegian Sweater, a good introduction to colour work (pattern on p. 60)*

Fig. 23

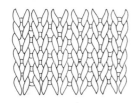

Stocking stitch

Stocking stitch is the name of the pattern obtained by placing all the smooth sides of the stitches on one side of the fabric which is used as the right side of the knitting (fig. 23), while all the looped stitches show on the other side or wrong side.

To achieve this, one row is worked by knitting all the stitches, and this is followed by a row in which all the stitches are purled. These two rows are repeated throughout all the fabric. Now that the distribution of the looped stitches is not even on both right and wrong sides the finished section will not lie flat but will tend to curl. Because of this curling tendency stocking stitch is usually edged with another pattern or a hem to produce a flat edge.

Reversed stocking stitch

Fig. 24

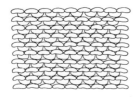

Although the purled side is commonly used as the wrong side of stocking stitch it comes into its own in many designs as the right side of the work, and when used in this way it is called reversed stocking stitch (fig. 24). It forms an interesting texture and is often used as a background fabric for a pattern which is predominantly smooth, thus creating a contrast between the two fabrics.

Ribbing

Fig. 25

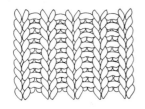

When stitches are worked alternately in knit and purl along a row with following rows placing all the smooth stitches above smooth stitches and looped stitches above looped stitches the result is a pattern of vertical lines which makes a very elastic fabric.

To experiment cast on 20 stitches. *Knit one stitch, purl one stitch, and repeat this from the * until all stitches are worked. Continue to repeat this row until the pattern can be seen (fig. 25).

This is called one and one rib and it forms a very useful elastic edge at lower edges of sweaters and cuffs, as well as being suitable for the entire garment.

Wider ribs can be made by placing the stitches in a different way. Two and two rib, with 2 stitches knitted and 2 purled alternately across the row is often used (fig. 26) and also a three

Fig. 26

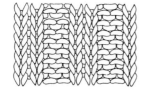

Opposite *Simple patterned Scarf Hood (pattern on p. 23) and Duffle Coat for toddler (pattern on p. 77)*

and three rib. The wider the panels of vertical stitches the less elastic the fabric will be.

These ribs have equal numbers of both types of stitches on either side of the fabric and although elastic are balanced and will not curl.

Variations of ribs, often used for the body of a garment above a more narrowly ribbed welt, can be unequally spaced as the rib in fig. 27.
Cast on a number of stitches divisible by 9.
1st row * Knit 4, purl 2, knit 1, purl 2, repeat from * to row end.
2nd row * Knit 2, purl 1, knit 2, purl 4, repeat from * to row end.

Repeat these 2 rows until there is sufficient pattern to show the effect.

Fig. 27

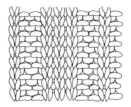

Flat fabrics

A quite different appearance from rib is achieved if the stitches are alternated instead of being arranged in vertical rows.

Moss stitch

This pattern will lie flat, is excellent for edges because the smooth and ridged stitches are evenly distributed on either side of the fabric and is usually called moss stitch, but in some areas is known as hit and miss stitch or in others as cats' teeth (fig. 28).
Cast on 21 stitches.
1st row Knit 1, * purl 1, knit 1, repeat from * to row end.
Repeat this row as required.

Fig. 28

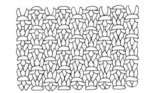

Basket stitch

Basket stitch has many variations but in its more simple forms it is only a step on from moss stitch. For basket stitch instead of alternating every stitch on every row small groups of similar stitches are placed together to form squares.
Cast on a number of stitches divisible by 6.
1st row * Knit 3, purl 3; repeat from * to row end.
2nd row Repeat row 1 and then work rows 1 and 2 once more.
5th row * Purl 3, knit 3, repeat from * to row end.
6th row Repeat the last row and then work the 5th row again followed by the 6th row once more.

Repeat these 8 rows to form a repeating all-over pattern of basket weave (fig. 29).

Fig. 29

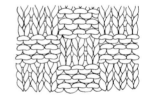

Horizontal ridges

Horizontal lines across the fabric make a simple pattern and are easily worked.

Wager welt

This is made by working 7 rows garter stitch (every row knit) followed by one purl row and then repeating these 8 rows. Coming between two knit or smooth rows the purl row makes more difference and a wider stripe than might be expected.

Ridged stocking stitch

Worked as for ordinary stocking stitch but every 6th row is knitted instead of being purled.

Project: Scarf Hood

A chunky hood can be knitted quickly with thick yarn and a broken rib pattern. Seam the scarf to form a hood for cold days or leave unstitched to wrap around. The pattern used makes a reversible fabric so there will be no wrong side showing.

Materials
The yarn is Patons Beehive Shetland-style Chunky
5×50 g balls
1 pair $6\frac{1}{2}$ mm needles
Measurements
Length approx 170 cm (68 in) unseamed
Tension
7 stitches and 9 rows to 5 cm worked on $6\frac{1}{2}$ mm needles

The method
Using $6\frac{1}{2}$ mm needles cast on 42 stitches.
1st row Knit 2, *purl 2, knit 2, repeat from * to row end.
2nd row Purl 2, *knit 2, purl 2, repeat from * to row end.
Repeat 1st and 2nd rows 3 times more.
9th row Purl 2, *knit 2, purl 2, repeat from * to row end.
10th row Knit 2, *purl 2, knit 2, repeat from * to row end.
Repeat 9th and 10th rows 3 times more.
Repeat from 1st row until work measures 65 cm then work rows 1 to 8 once.
Cast off.
To make up
DO NOT PRESS THIS YARN
Fold in half and seam from the centre for approx 25 cm to form hood. Darn in all ends.

Chapter 4

Making progress

Detailed working instructions are carefully prepared to assist knitters to make garments exactly
like the original design made by the designer.

Nothing that is not considered to be essential by
the yarn spinner or designer is included in the
instructions because space is valuable and is
used to give guidance or help only. Knitters do
not always treat the instructions with sufficient
respect and it is good to get into the habit of
always reading instructions *before* making a
garment, not after it has been spoilt by failure to
notice that it was yarn that should not have been
pressed, or that the pattern was read wrongly in
haste.

Instructions include the materials which will be
required, measurements of the finished garment,
the tension used in making the garment, any
notes of unusual abbreviations or yarn require-
ment for that particular design and the working
instructions with a guide to the final making up.

Materials

The yarn that is quoted in the materials section
should be obtained and used if at all possible.
Although it is possible in some cases to substitute other yarns (see Tension) the original
yarn is most suitable and is intended for use in the
particular design.

Measurements

It is usual to print instructions in several sizes so
that knitters have a range to choose from, but this
has to be achieved as economically as possible
without giving individual instructions for each
garment.

The most usual form is to print the sizes and
stitch numbers of the smallest design outside
brackets, with the remaining sizes in order within
the brackets. So four sizes beginning with an 85-
cm bust would read—85(90: 95: 100) cm. The

number of stitches to cast on would be given in the same way and it would be the knitter's task to select the chosen size each time figures or stitch numbers were shown. It is useful to pencil a mark by the chosen size throughout the instructions before beginning to knit. These marks can later be rubbed out so that no confusion is caused if another size is worked at some other time.

Tension

The key to producing a successful garment is found in the section on the leaflet headed 'tension'. Tension is expressed as the number of stitches and rows to a given measurement that was obtained in the original garment. To make a garment the same size and shape it is essential to obtain the same tension.

To check this it is necessary to make a sample swatch using the correct needles and yarn. Measure the swatch over at least 10 cm, first pressing it if the finished garment is to be pressed (see Pressing). It is important to measure over a reasonably large area because over less it is difficult to see whether it is a fraction of a stitch more or less than required and yet even fractions of stitches add together to make the final garment too small or too tight.

When there are too few stitches to the required measurement, change to finer needles and where there are too many stitches thicker needles are required. The actual needle size used does not matter in the least provided that the correct tension can be obtained with it.

Tension may be given as an exact tension over the particular stitch specified in the pattern or, for stitches which are difficult to measure, it may be given as a standard tension or a tension equivalent to a given figure. In both cases it means that provided the knitter can obtain the stated tension, which may be over stocking stitch although there is no stocking stitch in that particular design, then she should be able to obtain the particular tension required by the pattern. If a change of needle size has to be made to obtain the stocking stitch tension or stated tension then the same change must be made when working the pattern.

Abbreviations

Knitting instructions can take up a great deal of space unless many words are abbreviated. The knitters' vocabulary is not large and even beginners will find that they readily read K for knit and P for purl. Most abbreviations are in common use although styles of different leaflets and magazines may vary slightly.

The abbreviations used in this book are—

alt	alternate
beg	beginning
cm	centimetre(s)
cont	continue
dec	decrease
foll	following
g	gram(mes)
in	inch(es)
inc	increase
K	knit
K 2 tog	knit 2 stitches together
K-wise	knit-wise
M1	make 1 by lifting thread before next stitch, and working into back of it.
no	number
patt	pattern
psso	pass slipped stitch over
P	purl
P-wise	purl-wise
rem	remaining
rep	repeat
SKPO	sl 1, K 1, pass slipped stitch over
sl 1	slip 1
SSK	slip 2 stitches knitwise and knit tog

st	stitch(es)
st st	stocking stitch
tbl	through back(s) of loop(s)
tog	together
yb	yarn back
yf	yarn forward
yon	yarn over needle

Reading instructions

Read through all sections of the instructions before you knit to see that everything is understood. When there is something that is new or difficult to understand it is better to make sense of it before tackling the actual garment.

Asterisk signs

The asterisk * is placed before a group of words to denote that when repeats are to be worked it is from this point that the repeats start.

Brackets

Within a repeat there may be other stitches which themselves require to be repeated and they may be collected inside brackets with the number of times they are to be repeated stated after the final bracket. These brackets may be square [ ] where round brackets are used to group alternative sizes or they may be round ( ) if square brackets or oblique strokes — / / — are used for the various sizes.

Many repeats

A stitch pattern may use * to denote the point from which a repeat is made, but the same pattern may wish to denote that, for example, the raglan shaping on sleeves is to be worked in the same way as the shaping on a certain section of the back and in such a case both start and finish of the repeat would be marked by using **. Further sections would be marked by the addition of more asterisks either *** or possibly ****.

The instructions for projects given here carry the * as the repeat mark but any mark may be substituted and other symbols may be found in different publications.

Following instructions

Knit and purl stitches can combine to make interesting textures and abbreviated instructions make it quite simple to follow the pattern. If you are uncertain check with the abbreviation list on page 26.

Project: Pram rug

The pram rug uses moss stitch to make a border round a central checked pattern of purl stitches on a stocking stitch ground. Made in wool it can be pressed when finished and the edge with its even number of stitches on both sides of the fabric makes a border which will lie flat.

Materials
The yarn used is Patons Husky.
7 × 50 g balls.
1 pair of 6 mm needles.

Measurements
Approx. 57.5 by 75 cm (23 × 30 in) after pressing.

Tension
$7\frac{1}{2}$ sts and 10 rows to 5 cm, measured over st st worked on 6 mm needles.

The method
Using 6 mm needles and the thumb or cable method, cast on 85 sts.
1st row K 1, * P 1, K 1, rep from * to row end.
Rep 1st row 17 times more.

Begin pattern
1st row (K 1, P 1) 4 times, K to last 8 sts, (P 1, K 1) 4 times.
2nd row (K 1, P 1) 4 times, P to last 8 sts, (P 1, K 1) 4 times.
3rd row Work as 1st row.
4th row Work as 2nd row.
5th row (K 1, P 1) 4 times, K 3, * P 3, K 3, rep from * to last 8 sts, (P 1, K 1) 4 times.
6th row (K 1, P 1) 4 times, P 3, * K 3, P 3, rep from * to last 8 sts, (P 1, K 1) 4 times.
7th row Work as 5th row.
8th row Work as 6th row.
Rep rows 1–8 15 times more, then rows 1–4 once.
Next row K 1, * P 1, K 1, rep from * to row end.
Rep last row 17 times more.
Cast off.

To make up
Press on wrong side using a damp cloth and a warm iron. Darn in all ends.

Project: Overblouse

The chunky overblouse makes effective use of a narrow garter stitch line to divide the smoother panels of stocking stitch and introduces another pattern on the yoke which is emphasised by the edges of garter stitch. The neck edge is completed by a narrow section of ribbing for a neater finish.

Materials
The yarn used is Patons Husky.
12(13: 14)50 g balls.
1 pair each 5½ and 6½ mm needles.

Measurements
To fit an 85(90: 95) cm bust, 34(36: 38) in.
Length from shoulder: 60(61.25: 62.5) cm.
Sleeve seam: 40(40: 40) cm.

Tension
7 sts and 8 rows to 5 cm measured over st st worked on 6½ mm needles.

Back
Using 5½ mm needles cast on 69(73: 77) sts, using thumb or cable method.
K 4 rows.
Change to 6½ mm needles and ridged pattern as follows.
1st row K.
2nd row P.
Rep 1st and 2nd rows 3 times more.
9th row K.
10th row K.
Rep these 10 rows 6 times more.
K 4 rows.
Work yoke pattern:
1st row K.
2nd row P 1, * K 1, P 1, rep from * to row end.
3rd row K.
4th row P 2, * K 1, P 1, rep from * to last st, P 1.
Rep rows 1 to 4, 8(8: 9) times more, then rows 1 and 2, 0(1: 0) times.
K 1 row.
Work ribbed edging:
1st row P 1, * K 1, P 1, rep from * to row end.
2nd row K 1, * P 1, K 1, rep from * to row end.
Cast off in rib.

Front
Work as given for Back.

Sleeves (work 2 alike)
Using 5½ mm needles cast on 56 (58: 60) sts.

K 4 rows.
Change to $6\frac{1}{2}$ mm needles.
1st row K.
2nd row P.
Rep rows 1 and 2, 3 times more.
9th row K.
10th row K.
Rep rows 1 to 10, 6 times more.
K 4 rows.
Cast off.

To make up
Press pieces lightly on wrong side under a
damp cloth with a warm iron.
  Join ribbing at either side of neck for 10 cm at
each side. Sew cast-off edge of sleeve to either
side of main sections with shoulder seam in
centre of sleeve edge. Join side and sleeve
seams.

Chapter 5

Fig. 30

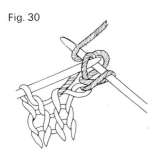

Shaping

Straight sections of knitting can be used for many items but to be able to shape exactly where required and in the way that is best gives a great deal more scope to the knitter. Shaping can be either increasing to give greater width or decreasing to reduce the number of stitches and the size of the section.

Simple increases

Fig. 31

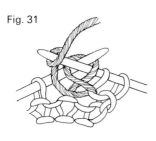

The easiest method of adding a stitch is to work twice into the same stitch, working into the front and the back of the same loop.
A knit increase To increase a knit stitch insert the right needle into the stitch, knit the stitch in the usual way but before removing the left needle knit into the back of the loop on the left needle to make an extra stitch (fig. 30).
A purl increase To increase a purl stitch work in the same way purling the first stitch and working the second stitch by purling into the back of the loop on the left needle before completing the two stitches (fig. 31).
This type of increase has many uses but is best at seam edges where the seam will cover it or where it is not easily noticed. It is also best worked one stitch before the end of the row and one stitch in from the beginning so that the edges are left as neat as possible—a great aid when it comes to sewing sections together.

Fig. 32

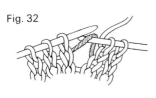

A neater, invisible increase

Fig. 33

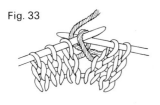

A more invisible increase, which does not alter the smooth line of the stitches, can be made in a different way. Lift the thread between the last stitch worked and the next to be worked using the tip of the right needle (fig. 32). Place the loop so gained on the left needle and knit or purl into the back of it (fig. 33). This forms an extra stitch and merges with the stitches around it. When worked without working into the back of the

31

loop the increase is less neat and forms a small openwork hole.

This increase is abbreviated to make 1 or M 1.

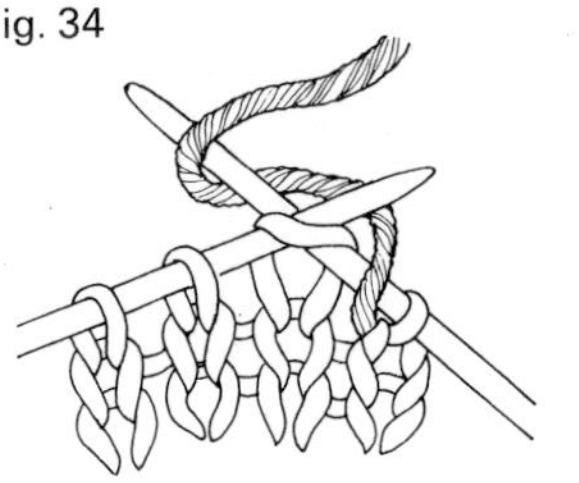

An openwork increase

This increase is often used for lace patterns where increased and decreased stitches are used to create a surface texture, but it also forms a decorative edging to a line of increasing and could be used on a raglan seam that is worked from the neck edge towards the lower edge, or a skirt panel worked waist to hem.

It is made by putting the yarn over the top of the right needle before working the next stitch (fig. 34). On the following row this strand is then knitted or purled becoming another stitch on the row. In this book it is referred to as a 'yarn over' increase and is abbreviated to y o n, standing for yarn over needle.

Between two knit stitches or a purl and knit stitch the yarn is placed over the top of the right needle and is then in the correct position for working the next stitch. However, when it is between a knit and purl stitch or two purl stitches the yarn must be put over the needle and taken round to the front. In some instructions separate abbreviations are given for each type but this can cause confusion and in all these projects it will be given as y o n.

Simple decrease

The simplest way of reducing two stitches to one and so decrease a stitch is to put the needle through two stitches and then work them in the usual way either by knitting or purling (fig. 35). This is abbreviated to K 2 tog or P 2 tog and can be used for more than one decrease. When it is intended to be over more stitches the number is indicated as K 3 tog, K 4 tog or K 5 tog, depending on whether 2, 3 or 4 stitches are to be decreased at the same time.

Pairing shaping

In decreasing as on a raglan seam it is necessary to see that each end of the work matches and if the decrease at the beginning slopes left in a similar direction to the seam the decrease used at the end of the row should slope to the right to correspond with that seam.

A K 2 tog decrease slopes to the right and is used at the end or left side of the work. To make a left-sloping decrease at the beginning of the row

Fig. 34

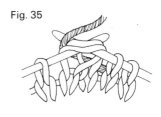

Fig. 35

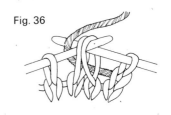

Fig. 36

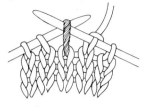

Fig. 37

it is usual to K 2 tog but working through the backs of the loops so that the stitches lie the reverse way (fig. 36). This is shown by adding tbl to the K 2 tog abbreviation.

Where decreases are worked on every row of stocking stitch the matching purl row will start with P 2 tog and finish with P 2 tog tbl.

A slipped decrease

A stitch is slipped when it is passed from one needle to the other without knitting or purling it (fig. 37). It is usual to keep the yarn behind the slipped stitch on the wrong side of the work. Stitches are slipped by inserting the needle into the stitch as if it was to be purled and then continuing to work along the row in the usual way. When it is necessary to slip a stitch knitwise it will always be indicated in the instructions by the addition of K-wise after sl 1.

Fig. 38

A slipped decrease sloping left is made by slipping one stitch, knitting the next stitch, then lifting the slipped stitch over the knitted stitch with the left needle tip and dropping it off the right needle (fig. 38). The abbreviation for this is SKPO or sl 1, K 1, psso.

In leaflets this decrease is sometimes teamed with a decrease made by knitting two stitches together at the end of the row but, correctly, the second decrease should be made in the following way.

Fig. 39

To work the right-sloping slipped decrease, knit one stitch and slip it back onto the left needle, with the right needle tip lift the stitch beyond it over the knitted stitch and off the left needle tip (fig. 39) before returning the knitted stitch to the right hand needle. It can be abbreviated to KSPO or K 1, sl 1, psso. Because it matches the SKPO it should always be used but is seldom used in instructions and so must be substituted by the knitter.

A substitute decrease

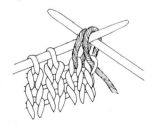

Fig. 40

This is a decrease which is seldom mentioned in instructions but can be used for a left-sloping decrease and is made very easily and is very neat when complete. Slip two stitches, one at a time, knit-wise onto the right needle. Insert the tip of the left needle through the front of both stitches together and knit as one stitch from this angle (fig. 40). This abbreviation is called SSK. This is one time when the stitches must be slipped knitwise.

A multiple decrease

Fig. 41

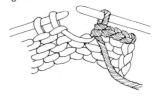

Where more than one stitch is to be decreased and is not required to slope to right or left a slipped decrease can be used.

Slip one stitch, K 2 tog, then lift the slipped stitch over the K 2 tog and off the right needle tip. This is abbreviated to SK2togPO or Sl 1, K 2 tog, psso.

An even larger decrease can be made by slipping extra stitches and knitting more stitches together before lifting the slipped stitches off the needle tip.

Large increases and decreases

Fig. 42

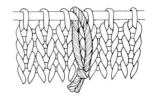

Where many stitches are required to be either added or subtracted at the side edge, it is best to cast these stitches on or off at the beginning of two rows (fig. 41).

Cast on or off at the right side, then complete the row and cast on or off at the beginning of the following row for the left-side shaping. The best way of casting on side stitches is to use the two-needle method.

Marker threads

Where a line of shaping is to be worked over a large number of rows it can be useful to mark the line with loops of contrast thread. This acts as a reminder that the shaping point has been reach-ed.

Make a loop of yarn with knotted ends. Before working the increase or decrease slip the loop onto the right needle. Work the next stitch in the usual way keeping the loop free from being worked in. On the following row slip the marker to the right needle and take care not to work it in. It can be moved up the work in this way and will keep the same position on each row. (Fig. 42.)

Adding shape

Shape is not only added by increasing and decreasing the number of stitches, it can be added by the direction the knitting takes.

Knitting a wedge

Darts require the formation of a wedge shape where the number of rows is greater at one edge of the work than at the other. This can be achieved by not working a full row but instead turning at some point in the row and working back to the edge. On the next row the work may be taken a few stitches further before the turn is made and then further still on the following row.

In this way a dart is formed over a given number

of stitches. The wedge is made by finding out how many stitches the dart is to cover and how many rows must be worked to give the required depth. On a width of fifty stitches a dart could be made over 20 rows if five more stitches were worked on every alternate row, or a more shallow dart could be formed by increasing to 10 stitches every alternate row giving a wedge of 10 rows.

To avoid leaving a hole at the point where the knitting is turned, work to the turning point and with the yarn forward slip the next stitch from left to right needle, turn the work and bringing the yarn round to the front slip the first stitch back to the needle in the right hand and work the remainder of the row.

By working wedge after wedge a flat circle of work is obtained and a full skirt can often be given shape in this way. (See also circular cushion, page 39.) Single wedges can be used to give greater depth to the backs of trousers and toddlers' leggings or to neatly fitting blouses where shoulder or bust darts are used for greater shaping.

The lines of knitted stitches can also be altered from horizontal to diagonal by placing increased or decreased stitches in groups spaced along the row to produce chevron effects (fig. 43) or at either end to create a single diagonal across the entire work as in the pattern for the Diagonal Top at the end of this chapter.

Diagonal lines can be made to radiate from a central point by working increasings on either side of a central stitch with decreases at either side edge to control the number of stitches. These must be worked to give the fabric its direction, not to increase or decrease stitches. Extra stitches must be added over and above these, if required to widen or narrow the work.

Fig. 43

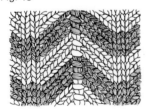

Project: Cushion

Adding shaping to knitting is no more difficult than knitting itself but it brings with it the possibility of making whatever you may want.

The cushion makes use of shaping to create geometric shapes which can be used as patchwork. Why stop at a cushion when you can add to this and make a bedspread or afghan? And there is no reason why patchwork can't be used for garments.

Materials

The yarn used is Patons Beehive Shetland Style Chunky.

3 × 50 g balls in mid shade A.

2 × 50 g balls in dark shade B.

1 × 50 g ball in light shade C.

1 pair 6 mm needles.

Cushion pad or stuffing.

Measurements

Approx. 31 by 44 cm ($12\frac{1}{2}$ × $17\frac{1}{2}$ in) when stuffed.

Tension

$7\frac{1}{2}$ sts and 12 rows to 5 cm measured over garter st worked on 6 mm needles.

Light squares

Using 6 mm needles and C cast on 1 st.

1st row K into front back and front of first st (3 sts).

2nd row K.

Cont in this way inc 1 st at each end of next and every alt row until there are 21 sts.

K 1 row.

Dec 1 st at each end of next and every alt row until 3 sts rem. K 1 row.

Last row K 3 tog, cut yarn and draw end through last st.

Work 3 more squares in same way.

Mid-colour shape

Using 6 mm needles and A cast on 1 st.

1st row K into front, back and front of first st (3 sts).

K 3 rows.

Cont to inc 1 st at each end of next and every 4th row until there are 21 sts.

K 3 rows.

Dec 1 st at each end of next and every alt row until 3 sts rem.

K 1 row.

Last row K 3 tog, cut yarn and draw through last st.

Work 7 more shapes in same way.

continued on page 39

Opposite *Three cushions using an exciting variety of unusual techniques. From top to bottom: Circular Cushion (pattern on p. 39); Striped Cushion (pattern on p. 58) and Patchwork Cushion (pattern on p. 35)*

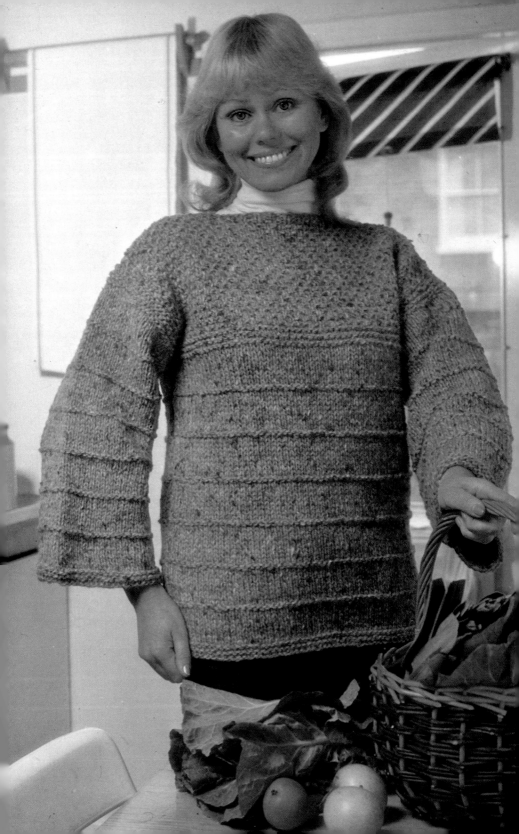

Dark-colour shape

Using 6 mm needles and B cast on 1 st.
1st row K into front, back and front of first st
(3 sts).
K 3 rows.
Cont to inc 1 st at each end of next and every
4th row until there are 21 sts.
K 3 rows.
Dec 1 st at each end of next and every 4th row
until 3 sts rem.
K 3 rows.
Last row K 3 tog, cut yarn and draw through
last st.

Work 3 more shapes in same way.

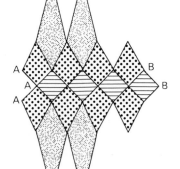

To make up

Join shapes as shown in diagram.
  When the shapes are joined fold point A to
join point B and complete the seam around the
4th light square. Complete the seams around
mid shape to form a tube. Fold in half so that 2
light squares are on back and 2 on front and
fold dark points over to complete the cushion,
leaving one seam open until pad or stuffing has
been added. Complete last seam.

Project: Cushion

This intriguing circular cushion makes use of the
knitting a wedge technique to achieve its round
shape.

Materials

The yarn used is Patons Beehive Shetland Type
Chunky.
2 × 50 g balls in each of 3 colours A, B, and C.
1 pair 6 mm needles.
Stuffing or pad.

Measurements

Approx 45 cm (18 in) in diameter.

Tension

$7\frac{1}{2}$ sts and 12 rows to 5 cm measured over
garter st worked on 6 mm needles.

Back

Using 6 mm needles and A cast on 30 sts.

Opposite *Easy Overblouse in ridged stocking
stitch with textured yoke (pattern on p. 29)*

1st row K.
2nd row K.
3rd row K 4, yf, sl 1, turn.
4th row With yf, sl 1, yb, K 4.
5th row K 8, yf, sl 1, turn.
6th row With yf, sl 1, yb, K 8.
7th row K 12, yf, sl 1, turn.
8th row With yf, sl 1, yb, K 12.
9th row K 16, yf, sl 1, turn.
10th row With yf, sl 1, yb, K 16.
11th row K 20, yf, sl 1, turn.
12th row With yf, sl 1, yb, K 20.
13th row K 24, yf, sl 1, turn.
14th row With yf, sl 1, yb, K 24.
15th row K 28, yf, sl 1, turn.
16th row With yf, sl 1, yb, K 28.
Work 13th and 14th rows, 11th and 12th rows,
9th and 10th rows, 7th and 8th rows, 5th and
6th rows, 3rd and 4th rows, and 1st and 2nd
rows once more in that order.
Cut the yarn leaving an end to darn in.
Rep these 30 rows with B and then C and then
with A, B and C 3 times more to complete the
circle.
Cast off.

Front
Work as given for Back.
To make up
Join cast off and on edges of each circle. Run a
thread through centre stitches and draw up.
   Place right sides of circles together and seam
around edges leaving a gap for the stuffing or a
cushion pad. Turn right side out, stuff and
complete seam.
DO NOT PRESS THIS YARN.

Project: Doll

This doll is very easily made as most of the
sections are straight but a few rows of shaping
will allow you to try out both making and
decreasing stitches. For a young child the hair
style must be serviceable but for an older child
spend a little extra time adding a stylish plait or
dainty ringlets.
Materials
The yarn used is Patons Trident Double
Knitting.
1 × 25 g ball of each colour, cream (A), red (B),
blue (C), and brown (D).
1 pair each $3\frac{3}{4}$ and 4 mm needles.

Stuffing.
Scraps of black and white felt for eyes.
Red and brown embroidery cotton for face.

Measurements
Approx 45 cm (18 in) high when finished.

Tension
11 sts and 15 rows to 5 cm measured over st st worked on 4 mm needles.

Legs (work 2 alike)
Using $3\frac{3}{4}$ mm needles and A cast on 20 sts.
Work in st st beg with a K row.
Work 4 rows A, 4 rows B alt, carrying the colour not in use up the side of the leg, twisting it with the colour in use on the 3rd row of each stripe.
Work until the 8 stripe rows have been repeated 7 times (8 red stripes worked) then work 4 rows more in A.
Cast off.
Fold legs into tubes and stuff lightly.

Body (work 2 alike)
Using $3\frac{3}{4}$ mm needles and B cast on 26 sts.
Work in st st beg with a K row.
Work 36 rows.

Shape shoulders
Cast off 4 sts at beg ofnext 4 rows.
Change to A for neck and face.
1st row K 10.
2nd row P.
Rep rows 1 and 2 twice.
5th row (K 1, M 1) 3 times, K 4 (M 1, K 1) 3 times (16 sts).
6th row P.
7th row (K 1, M 1) 5 times, K 6, (M 1, K 1) 5 times (26 sts).
8th row P.
Work 18 rows without shaping.
Next row (K 1, K 2 tog) 3 times, K 8, (K 2 tog, K 1) 3 times (20 sts).
Work 3 rows.
Next row K 2 tog, * K 1, K 2 tog, rep from * to end (13 sts). P 1 row.
Last row K 1, * K 2 tog, rep from * to end.
Cast off.
  Join 2 sections together leaving lower edge open until stuffed, then seam. Sew legs to either side of lower edge.

Arms (work 2 alike)
Using $3\frac{3}{4}$ mm needles and B, cast on 17 sts.
Work in st st beg with a K row.

Work 26 rows.

K 4 rows.

Change to A for hands.

1st row K 1, * K 2 tog, K 3, K 2 tog, K 1, rep from * once (13 sts).

Work 7 rows st st.

Last row K 1, * K 2 tog, rep from * to end.

Cut yarn and thread through rem sts.

Fold arms in half and seam from tip to cast on edge. Stuff and sew to either side of shoulders.

Dress (work 2 alike)

Using 4 mm needles and C cast on 54 sts.

K 4 rows.

Work in st st beg with a K row.

Work 28 rows.

Shape yoke

1st row * K 2 tog, rep from * to end (27 sts).

K 6 rows.

Divide for neck.

1st row K 7, cast off 13 sts, K 7.

Work front shoulder on these last 7 sts.

K 15 rows.

Cast off.

With right side of work facing rejoin yarn to rem 7 sts for other shoulder.

K 15 rows.

Cast off.

Press pieces under a damp cloth with a warm iron, avoiding the yoke.

Join shoulder and side seams.

Shoes (work 2 alike)

Using 3¾ mm needles and C cast on 9 sts.

K 36 rows.

Cast off.

Sew cast on edge to back of leg. Fold shoe and sew cast off edge to front of leg. Seam folded sides after stuffing front of shoe lightly.

To complete

Wind yarn D around head to form hair, sewing along top and back of head with back stitch to form parting.

Cut 18 lengths of yarn approx 45 cm long. Knot together at one end. Divide into 3 groups and plait. Knot other end. Form plait into a circle and sew to top of head with tail hanging forward over one shoulder.

Alternatively make a plait with strands 30 cm long, form into a circle and sew to top of head.

Make each ringlet by cutting a strand approx 40 cm long. Knot ends and holding the knotted end in one hand, place a finger of the other hand into the loop, hold it taut and turn finger until the two strands are tightly twisted together. Without removing finger, bring both ends of the rope together, remove finger and knot ends before allowing strands to twist.

Sew knots of each ringlet to centre of plait so that the ringlets fall over the knots and hide them. Ringlets can be made all one length or the length can be varied. Trim with a tie of ribbon or yarn.

Thread shoes with a lace of yarn. Cut felt eyes and sew in place. Embroider eyebrows and mouth.

Project: Pleated skirt

A pleated skirt can be made with swirls of three dimensional pleats, either with the fullness being made by the same technique as used for the circular cushion or with the fullness and pleats worked together in gores.

Materials
The yarn used is Patons Double Knitting Wool.
4 (5: 6) 50 g balls.
1 pair each $3\frac{3}{4}$ and 4 mm needles.
Waist length elastic 2.5 cm wide.

Measurements
To fit 60 (65: 70) cm chest size 24 (26: 28) in.
Length: 30 (35: 40) cms.

Tension
11 sts and 15 rows to 5 cm measured over st st worked on 4 mm needles.

Back
Using 4 mm needles cast on 198 (212: 226) sts.
K 4 rows.
5th row K 2, * P 5, K 2, rep from * to end.
6th row P 2, * K 5, P 2, rep from * to end.
Work 5th and 6th rows 4 (5: 6) times more.
Next row K 2, * P 2, P 2 tog, P 1, K 2, rep from * to end.
Next row P 2, * K 4, P 2, rep from * to end.
Next row K 2, * P 4, K 2, rep from * to end.
Next row P 2, * K 4, P 2, rep from * to end.
Rep last 2 rows 4 (5: 6) times more.
Next row K 2, * P 1, P 2 tog, P 1, K 2, rep from * to end.
Next row P 2, * K 3, P 2, rep from * to end.
Next row K 2, * P 3, K 2, rep from * to end.
Next row P 2, * K 3, P 2, rep from * to end.
Rep last 2 rows 4 (5: 6) times more.

Next row K 2, * P 1, P 2 tog, K 2, rep from * to end.
Next row P 2, * K 2, P 2, rep from * to end.
Next row K 2, * P 2, K 2, rep from * to end.
Next row P 2, * K 2, P 2, rep from * to end.
Rep last 2 rows 7 (8:9) times more.
Next row K 2, * P 2 tog, K 2, rep from * to end.
Next row P 2, * K 1, P 2, rep from * to end.
Next row K 2, * P 1, K 2, rep from * to end.
Next row P 2, * K 1, P 2, rep from * to end.
Rep last 2 rows 9 times more.
Change to 3¾ mm needles.
Next row K 2 tog, * P 1, K 2 tog, rep from * to end.
Next row P 1, * K 1, P 1, rep from * to end.
Next row K 1, * P 1, K 1, rep from * to end.
Rep last 2 rows 3 times more.
Cast off.
Work 2nd piece for Front as given for Back.

To make up
Seam pieces down sides using an invisible seam.

Work casing stitch around inside of K 1, P 1 rib and thread with circle of elastic.

Press seams and remainder of skirt lightly as required.

Project: Diagonal top

Shaping is not only intended for horizontal knitting. This top is shaped in two ways at the same time, one to achieve the diagonal effect and the second to make the required shape.

Materials
The yarn used is Jaeger Lambswool.
2 × 50 g balls in main shade A.
2 × 50 g balls in 1st contrast, B.
3 × 50 g balls in 2nd contrast, C.
1 pair 4½ mm needles.

Measurements
To fit an 80 (85: 90: 95) cm bust, 32 (34: 36: 38) in.
Length from shoulder: 55 cm.

Tension
9 sts and 16 rows to 5 cm measured over garter st worked on 4½ mm needles.

Back
Using 4½ mm needles and A cast on 1 st.
1st row K into front, back and front of st (3 sts).
K 1 row.

3rd row K 1, K twice into thread before next st, K 1, K twice into thread before next st, K 1 (7 sts).
K 1 row.
5th row K 1, M 1, K 2, M 1, K 1, M 1, K 2, M 1, K 1 (11 sts).
6th and every even row K.
7th row K 1, M 1, K 4, M 1, K 1, M 1, K 4, M 1, K 1.
9th row K 1, M 1, K 6, M 1, K 1, M 1, K 6, M 1, K 1.
11th row K 1, M 1, K 8, M 1, K 1, M 1, K 8, M 1, K 1.
Cont in this way inc 4 sts on every odd row, placing inc after 1st st, on either side of centre st, and before last st.
Work until there are 111 (119: 127: 135) sts.
K 1 row.

Shape sides
Next row K 2 tog tbl, K to centre st and M 1 on either side of centre st, K to last 2 sts, K 2 tog.
K 1 row.
Cont rep these 2 rows once and then rep them using B for 2 rows and A for two rows 9 times.
 Rep these 2 rows using B for 8 rows then rep same rows using C for 2 rows and B for 2 rows alternately 6 times in all.
Using C only rep last 2 rows until centre work measures 55 cm or required total length.
Next row K to one stitch before centre st, K 2 tog, K 2 tog tbl, K to last 2 sts, K 2 tog.
 Complete one side first leaving sts at other side of centre st on a holder. K 1 row.
Next row K 2 tog tbl. K to last 2 sts, K 2 tog.
Rep last 2 rows until 2 sts remain. K 2 tog and draw yarn through. Rejoin yarn to centre edge of rem sts and work in same way.
Work front in same way.

To make up
Join shoulder seams leaving neck opening and join side seams below armholes.

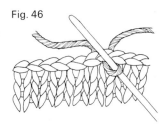

Chapter 6

Edges and buttonholes

Bands to edge openings, collars to trim neck edges and other finishing touches can be made separately and sewn onto the garment but the amount of making up can be reduced by picking up stitches from a knitted edge and working the next section directly into place.

Picking up stitches

Borders and edges are often worked on a needle size that is finer than that used for the actual garment, but stitches are most easily picked up with a needle one size finer than the border size.

Fig. 46

The most important factors in obtaining a neat edge are never to pick up a new stitch through a very loose loop or to work so close to the edge that only one loop of a stitch is used, even when it is the cast on or off edge.

Pick up stitches with the right side of the section facing and insert the needle through both strands of the first stitch (fig. 46). Loop the yarn from the ball round the right needle and draw a loop through as for a knit stitch. Insert the right needle through the next stitch, put the yarn round the right needle and draw a loop through, repeating until the required number of stitches have been picked up.

Spacing

Never attempt to pick up stitches along an edge without first dividing it into even sections with pins. Even an experienced knitter is unlikely to finish the edge without packing stitches in at the end or having too few stitches to complete. It is easier to pick up 10 stitches from 5 sections than to pick up 50 stitches evenly along an edge.

Fig. 47

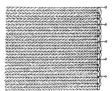

Shaped edges

On cast on or off edges both loops of the stitches must be picked up and on side edges a complete stitch should be picked up, keeping in line with the row, because stitches out of line will detract from a neat, tailored finish.

On inward curves space the stitches so that there are fewer at the centre of the curve, while on an outward curve more are required at the centre of the curve. When all the stitches required are on one needle, change to using the correct size for the section being worked.

Buttonholes

The making of small or large buttonholes need present no problems.

Small buttonholes

The quickest method of making a small buttonhole suitable for fine knitting, such as in babies' and toddlers' garments, is to work two stitches together followed by a yarn over needle increase. This retains the correct number of stitches and when the 'yon' is worked in the following row a small neat hole is left in the fabric (fig. 48).

Horizontal buttonholes

Instructions for making buttonholes usually state that a given number of stitches should be cast off on one row and the same number cast on above the cast off stitches in the following row. This forms a buttonhole but tends to leave the knitter with a loose loop at one end of the hole which spoils the appearance and is unnecessary if the hole is worked by the substitute method suggested here.

Perfect buttonholes

Work until the buttonhole position is reached. Bring the yarn to the front of the work, slip the next stitch from left to right needle and take the yarn round to the back of the work. Leave the yarn hanging at the back until required. Using the left needle tip lift the first slipped stitch over the second and off the right needle tip to make the first cast off stitch (fig. 49). * Slip the next stitch on the left needle to the right and lift the stitch before it over and off the needle tip to give the second cast off stitch. Repeat from * for the number of stitches to be cast off. Slip last loop on right back to left needle.

Turn the work and pick up the hanging yarn, taking it between the needles to the back of the work. Insert the right needle into the stitch on the left needle and using the cable method cast on one more stitch than was cast off, bringing the yarn to the front before slipping the last stitch to be cast on to the left needle (fig. 50).

Turn the work and slip the first stitch on the left needle to the right, lifting the stitch before it over the slipped stitch and off the tip of the right needle, leaving the correct number of stitches

Fig. 48

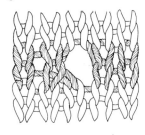

Fig. 49

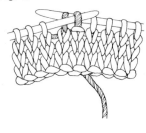

Fig. 50

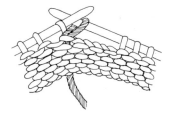

and the work ready to be completed to the end of the row.

When working buttonholes on stocking stitch work the hole on a purl row to make a neater right side.

Picked up button bands

Horizontal buttonholes worked on a band that is picked up along a front edge and worked outwards will appear to be vertical holes lying in the opposite direction to the usual horizontal hole. But true vertical buttonholes can be made in a different way as the work is knitted upwards or downwards.

Vertical buttonholes

Work to the buttonhole position and turn, leaving the remaining stitches on a holder or spare needle. Work on the first set of stitches until the buttonhole is the required length, then leave this section and rejoin the yarn at the base of the buttonhole on the other side (fig. 51). Work to correspond with the first side, then continue to work across both sections together until the next buttonhole position is reached.

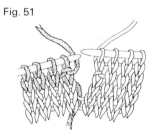

Fig. 51

Strengthening buttonholes

The method given for horizontal buttonholes produces a neat hole that will withstand wear but all buttonholes can be strengthened, both to give better wear and to retain shape. Use a fine cotton or silk for wool or a synthetic yarn for all man-made fibres and work buttonhole stitch around the two longer sides (fig. 52). Small buttonholes can also be strengthened by working a tiny circle of blanket stitch around the hole.

On the button side of the opening, a small disc or button sewn behind the actual button will save soft knitted fabrics from being pulled out of shape. The threads through the button are taken directly through the small button as well and this prevents stitches from pulling against the knitting.

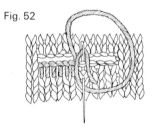

Fig. 52

Project: Bootees

Bootees for a baby are delightful to knit, small enough to finish quickly but give the opportunity to try tiny buttonholes which are used as ribbon slotting round the ankle. They also offer a chance to try picking up stitches along the side of the foot and can be trimmed with a few embroidery stitches.

Materials

The yarn used is Patons Fairytale Quickerknit.
1 × 20 g ball.
1 pair 3¾ mm needles.
Length of narrow ribbon.
Embroidery cotton.

Measurements

To fit birth to 3 months.

Tension

13 sts and 17 rows to 5 cm measured over st st worked on 3¾ mm needles.

The method

Begin at top edge and using 3¾ mm needles cast on 36 sts.
1st row * K 1, P 1, rep from * to end.
Rep 1st row 20 times more.
Next row K.
Ribbon slotting row K 2 tog, * yon, K 2 tog, rep from * to end.
Next row K.

Divide for instep

1st row K 23, turn, P 11, leave rem 12 sts at either side of central 11 sts on holders.

Work instep

1st row K.
2nd row P.
Rep rows 1 and 2, 7 times more. Cut yarn leaving an end to darn in.
   With right side of work facing K 12 sts from holder at right side of instep, pick up and K 10 sts along right side of instep. Work across 11 sts of instep thus – K 2 tog, K 7, K 2 tog – pick up and K 10 sts down other side of instep and K 12 sts from rem holder (53 sts).
K 9 rows.

Shape sole

1st row K 1, * K 2 tog tbl, K 21, K 2 tog, K 1, rep from * once (49 sts).
2nd, 4th, 6th and 8th rows K.
3rd row K 1, * K 2 tog tbl, K 19, K 2 tog, K 1, rep from * once (45 sts).
5th row K 1, * K 2 tog tbl, K 17, K 2 tog, K 1, rep from * once (41 sts).
7th row K 1, * K 2 tog tbl, K 15, K 2 tog, K 1, rep from * once (37 sts).
9th row K 1, * K 2 tog tbl, K 13, K 2 tog, K 1, rep from * once (33 sts).
Cast off.
Make 2nd bootee in same way.

To make up

Sew up the seam at back, heel, and sole of bootee.

Thread ribbon through slotting to tie at centre front.

Embroider centre front of instep.

Project: Slippers

Materials

The yarn used is Patons Fairytale Quickerknit.

1 × 20 g ball.

1 pair $3\frac{3}{4}$ mm needles.

Narrow ribbon.

Measurements

To fit birth to 3 months.

Tension

13 sts and 17 rows to 5 cm over st st worked on $3\frac{3}{4}$ mm needles.

The method

Using $3\frac{3}{4}$ mm needles cast on 27 sts.

1st row K 1, * P 1, K 1, rep from * to end.

Rep 1st row 13 times more.

Ribbon slotting row K 1, * yon, K 2 tog, rep from * to end.

Begin sides

1st row Cast on 8 sts, K to end.

2nd row Cast on 8 sts, K to end.

3rd row Inc, K to last st, inc.

4th row K.

Rep 3rd and 4th rows 3 times.

Cast off 21 sts at beg of next 2 rows.

K 60 rows on rem 9 sts.

Last row K 1, * yon, K 2 tog, rep from * to end of row.

Cast off.

To make up

Join ribbon slotting on narrow strip to slotting at either side of cuff. Sew strip along either side of foot, up shaped section and to ribbon slotting.

Thread ribbon through slots.

Chapter 7

Adding colour

Colour can be introduced into knitting in various ways and can bring a new look to a well-liked design that has been worked previously in a self-colour.

Stripes
Whether wide, narrow, regular or random, stripes mean little extra work other than that of choosing the colours to be used. The colours are joined in in the same way as a new ball of yarn, at the side edge, leaving ends to be darned in when making up.

Narrow stripes

Fig. 53

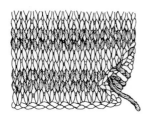

When stripes are not very wide the colours not in use can be carried up the side of the work. At the side edge twist the yarn in use round the other colours or colour before starting a new row. The yarn will hold the unused colours up to the point where a colour change is made and the new colour will then form the same lock each time it returns to the side of the work (fig. 53).

Wide stripes
Wide stripes can be worked with the yarn not in use carried up the side but the seams will be less bulky if the yarn is cut and left to be darned in later at the end of each stripe.

Smooth stripes
Stripes on stocking stitch will have smooth edges no matter on which row the yarn change is made. When working garter stitch if the yarn is joined on a wrong side row and on any row in reversed stocking stitch the join will show as a row of loops against the previous colour. Thought by some knitters to be 'wrong', this feature can be incorporated into the design and provides a way of varying stripes and gives a more gradual or shaded edge.

Ribbing will always show these loops on the purled stitches but this can be remedied by working the yarn-joining row as a knit row on the right side of the fabric, reverting to the rib for all other rows. This can be seen in the striped stockings where each colour is begun with a knit row.

Vertical stripes

Less often used than horizontal stripes, vertical stripes are quite simple to work and are more economical with yarn than some forms of coloured work. If one ball is used for each stripe no extra yarn is required because the colours are twisted together at the point where they join, both saving yarn and holding the edge stitches together without gaps.

Work the first row by joining in one ball of each colour required as the stripe position is reached.

On the next row, work the first stripe and when ready to use the second colour hold the first colour to the left over the top of the colour that is about to be used. Lift up the second colour and bring it up from under the first colour ready to work the stitch. It will hold the first colour in place until the following row.

It makes no difference whether the work is knitted or purled, each join is laid over the following colour which is brought up and round leaving no slack loop (fig. 54). The yarn must be changed on the wrong side of the fabric, so for stocking stitch the yarn will be crossed on the back on knit rows and on the front for purl rows.

This method can be used wherever the area of colour makes it practical and is neater than stranding the yarn across the back of the work.

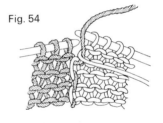

Fig. 54

Fairisle knitting

Fairisle knitting is a particular technique applied to a certain type of design and is not just any geometric banded pattern that is knitted in many colours.

The designs are usually worked in bands, not necessarily all over the garment, and although many colours may be used, only two are used on any one row, the background often being shaded as well as the design on it.

The two colours in use are used regularly along the row never having too many stitches of one colour. Either colour when not actually in use on any row is carried across the back of the work until it is required again. The other colours are left at the side and carried up until required, as when working stripes. The method of carrying the alternate colour is called stranding and forms fairly even, loose loops on the wrong side of the fabric (fig. 55). Loops pulled tightly from one

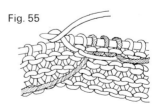

Fig. 55

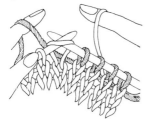

Fig. 56

colour to the next will cause puckering and loops left too wide will cause the stitches to separate and leave gaps.

The islanders who use this type of knitting have the answer to controlling the flow of the yarns and producing smooth regular fabrics. They combine the British way of knitting with the yarn round the forefinger of the right hand with the second colour Continental style over the forefinger of the left hand (fig. 56). In this way they do not have to lay down one yarn to pick up the other but use their fingers to flick the colours into place alternately.

Fairisle knitting is at its easiest when worked on sets of double-pointed needles or circular needles for in knitting round the right side of the work is always facing the knitter and the pattern can be seen as it is worked. Worked on two needles the stranding hides the pattern on the wrong side rows and results in the knitter having to turn the work to check the pattern.

Following instructions

Fairisle knitting is always worked in stocking stitch as the smooth surface shows the coloured patterning to best advantage.

Instructions are seldom written row for row because they are then difficult to read, not from the words, but because there are so many numbers and symbols. Instead they are usually supplied in a visual chart form. On this each colour is allocated a letter or symbol printed as a key on the chart.

The rows are numbered and it is usual to find odd rows are knit rows and even rows are purl unless, of course, the work is circular. Odd rows are read from right to left, but when the work is turned for the purl row the chart cannot also be turned and so is read from left to right.

It is usual to show one pattern repeat, which is often bracketed as in the chart. Designs are frequently placed so that the pattern is central. To achieve this, extra stitches may be shown at the side of the repeat. The knitter would continue repeating the bracketed stitches as often as they will divide into the total number of stitches, completing the row by working the edge stitches as shown in the instructions.

When instructions are written fully the symbol for knit and purl is printed only once at the beginning of the row and is followed by a letter representing a colour as it is used with the number of stitches to be worked in that colour preceding it thus—

K 4A, * 2 B, 1 A, 1 B, 1 A, 2 B, 5 A, rep from * to last 11 sts, 2 B, 1 A, 1 B, 1 A, 2 B, 4 A.

Fig. 57

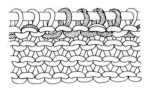

Jacquard knitting

The alternative method to stranding is called weaving and is suitable for use with two or more colours where the colours are used frequently across the row.

Instead of being looped across the back of the work they are continually twisted around themselves keeping a close mesh of the yarns on the wrong side of the fabric. The colour being carried is laid across the top of the needle so that the yarn working the next stitch catches it only on the wrong side, and does not take it through to the front. Although this makes for a neat wrong side and fewer loops to catch in wear, it does have a tendency to make for a less smooth surface (fig. 57).

Project: Socks

The patterns which follow show two different ways of using colour and begin to explore the many possibilities that even simple designs present. The striped socks are worked in an elastic rib to give a neat fit with every 4th row being knitted to give a smooth colour join at either side of the stripes. Worked on two needles the socks are seamed down the centre back and on either side of the foot.

Materials

The yarn used is Patons Trident Double Knitting.
3 × 25 g balls of A, purple.
2 × 25 g balls of B, emerald.
2 × 25 g balls of C, blue.
2 × 25 g balls of D, red.
1 pair each $3\frac{1}{4}$ and $3\frac{3}{4}$ mm needles.

Measurements

To fit an average adult leg.
Length to top of heel: 36 cm or as required.

Tension

Equivalent to $11\frac{1}{2}$ sts and $15\frac{1}{2}$ rows to 5 cm measured over st st worked on $3\frac{3}{4}$ mm needles.

continued on page 57

Opposite *Pram Rug (pattern on p. 28) and two cuddly soft toys, the Doll (p. 40) and Lion (p. 100)*

The method
Using $3\frac{1}{4}$ mm needles and A cast on 58 sts. (If desired the invisible method of casting on can be used, see page 120.)

1st row K 2, * P 2, K 2, rep from * to end.

2nd row P 2, * K 2, P 2, rep from * to end.

Rep last 2 rows once more.

Leave A at side of work and join in B.

5th row K.

6th row Work as given for 2nd row.

7th row Work as given for 1st row.

8th row Work as given for 2nd row.

Change to $3\frac{3}{4}$ mm needles.

Rep last 4 rows, working in stripes of 4 rows C, D, A and B.

Work until leg measures 36 cm or required length to top of heel, ending with a wrong side row.

Divide for heel
Slip first 13 and last 13 sts onto one needle with centre back opening in centre and have rem sts on holder.

With right side facing and A work first row thus, closing the back opening from this point.

1st row Sl 1 knitwise, K 11, K 2 tog, K 12.

2nd row Sl 1 purlwise, P to end.

3rd row Sl 1 knitwise, * K 1, with yb sl 1 purlwise, rep from * to last 2 sts, K 2, K to end.

Rep 2nd and 3rd rows 10 times more, then 2nd row once.

Turn heel
1st row K 15, sl 1, K 1, psso, turn.

2nd row P 6, P 2 tog, turn.

3rd row K 7, sl 1, K 1, psso, turn.

4th row P 8, P 2 tog, turn.

Cont in this way until all sts have been worked across, ending with a P row. Cut yarn.

Shape instep
With right side of heel facing and A, pick up and K 12 sts along side of heel, K 15 sts across heel and K up 12 sts down other side of heel.

1st row P.

2nd row K 1, K 2 tog tbl, K to last 3 sts, K 2 tog, K 1.

3rd row P.

Rep last 2 rows until 23 sts rem.

Cont in st st until foot measures approx 5 cm less than the required finished foot length to

---

Opposite V-necked Sweater with decorative border (pattern on p. 93) worn with the Pleated Skirt (pattern on p. 43)

toe, ending with a P row.
Shape toe
1st row K 1, K 2 tog tbl, K to last 3 sts, K 2 tog, K 1.
2nd row P.
Rep last 2 rows until 11 sts rem.
Leave sts on holder to graft with other side or cast off if preferred.

With right side of work facing, rejoin yarn to rem sts and cont in stripe patt until instep measures same as foot to start of toe shaping, ending with a right side row.
Last striped row P 1, K 2, * P 2 tog, K 2, rep from * to last st, P 1 (23 sts). Cut yarn.
Shape toe
With right side facing and A work as for other side.
To make up
Join back seam to heel. Seam both sides of instep, grafting toe stitches together or seaming if they have been cast off.

Project: Striped cushion

This cushion is quick to knit and gives a good opportunity both for chart reading and for using the method of colour changing described for vertical stripes. The result is a professionally worked wrong side and a cushion cover where the colours join without gaps and irregular stitches.
Materials
The yarn used is Patons Beehive Shetland-style Chunky.
1 × 50 g ball in main shade A.
2 × 50 g balls in 1st contrast B.
2 × 50 g balls in 2nd contrast C.
1 pair 6 mm needles.
Stuffing or pad for cushion.
Measurements
Approx 40 cm by 30 cm (16 by 12 in) when finished.
Tension
7 sts and 10 rows to 5 cm measured over st st worked on 6 mm needles.
Note
Divide each ball into half so that each colour section can be worked with a separate ball.

Back

Using 6 mm needles and A cast on 58 sts.

1st row K 12A, leave A hanging and join in B, K 12B, leave B hanging and join in 2nd ball of A, K 10A, leave A hanging and join in C, K 14C, leave C hanging and join in 2nd ball of B, K 10B.

2nd row P 10B, pass B over end of C and bring C up, P 14C, pass C over end of A and bring A up, P 10A, pass A over end of B and bring B up, P 12B, pass B over end of A and bring A up, P 12A.

3rd row K 12A, pass A over B and bring B up, K 12B, pass B over A and bring A up, K 10A, pass A over C and bring C up, K 14C, pass C over B and bring B up, K 10B.

Cont working from the chart bearing in mind that each small square along a line represents a stitch and each line upwards stands for one row. When the chart has been worked cast off using one colour.

Key ☐ Cream A
     ◉ Dark B
     ☒ Mid C

Rep rows 31 and 32 14 times more

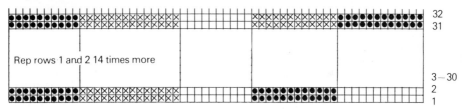

32
31

Rep rows 1 and 2 14 times more

3 – 30
2
1

Front

Work as given for Back.

To make up

Press on the wrong side under a damp cloth with a warm iron.

Place right sides together and join the side seams and one long seam.

Turn out to the right side, stuff and complete final seam.

Project: Norwegian sweater

Coloured knitting is always popular and this Norwegian-type sweater involves just the right amount of work to make it suitable for those who have not tried their hand at this type of technique before.

Materials

The yarn used is Jaeger Mix n' Match Double Knitting wool.

9 (9:10:10) 50 g balls of main shade, A.

3 (3:3:3) 50 g balls in 1st contrast, B.

1 (1:1:1) 50 g ball in 2nd contrast, C.

1 pair each $3\frac{1}{4}$ and 4 mm needles.

Measurements

To fit an 80 (85: 90: 95) cm, 32 (34: 36: 38) in bust/chest.

Length to shoulder: 63.75 (65: 66.25: 67.5) cm.

Sleeve seam: 42.5 (42.5: 45: 45) cm.

Tension

11 sts and 15 rows to 5 cm measured over st st worked on 4 mm needles.

Back

Using $3\frac{1}{4}$ mm needles and B cast on 90 (94: 102: 106) sts.

Work 5 cm in K 2, P 2, rib with K 2 at each end of right side rows, and inc 7 (9: 7: 9) sts on last row. 97 (103: 109: 115) sts.

Change to 4 mm needles.

** Using A work 4 rows st st, beg with a K row.

Using C work 2 rows st st, beg with a K row.

Using B K 2 rows.

Using A work 2 rows st st, beg with a K row.

Using C K 2 rows.

Using A work 2 rows st st, beg with a K row.

Next row K 1A, * 1 B, 1 A, rep from * to end.

Next row P 1B, * 1 A, 1 B, rep from * to end.

**.

Cont using A only and working in st st until side seam measures 42.5 cm or required length to armhole, ending with a P row.

Shape armholes

Place marker threads at ends of last row.

Using B K 2 rows.

Using A work 2 rows st st, beg with a K row.

Using C K 2 rows.

Using A work 2 rows st st, beg with a K row.

Using B K 2 rows.

Using A work 2 rows st st, beg with a K row.

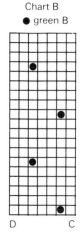

Chart A
★ red, C

Chart B
● green B

D   C

Place design from chart A on next row thus—
Using A K 6 (7: 8: 9) sts, * work 13 sts from
chart A as shown, K 5 (6: 7: 8) with A, rep
from * 4 times more, to last st, K 1 A.
Work next 12 rows from chart in this way as
placed.
Using A only work 2 rows st st, beg with a
P row.
Using B K 2 rows.
Using A work 2 rows st st, beg with a P row.
Using C, P 2 rows.
Using A work 2 rows st st, beg with a P row.
Using B P 2 rows.
Using A work 3 rows st st, beg with a P row.
Cont in st st without shaping working from
chart B working from C to D along row until 1st
rems as shown on chart.
Cont until work measures 60 (61.25: 62.5:
63.75) cm ending with a P row.
Shape shoulders
Cast off 6 (6: 7: 7) sts at beg of next 2 rows.
Cast off 6 (7: 7: 7) sts at beg of next 2 rows.
Cast off 6 (7: 7: 8) sts at beg of next 2 rows
and 7 (7: 7: 8) sts at beg of next 2 rows.
Cast off 7 (7: 8: 8) sts at beg of next 2 rows
and leave 33 (35: 37: 39) rem sts on holder for
neck.

Front
Work as given for Back until 16 rows less than
Back to shoulder, ending with a P row.
Divide for neck
1st row Keeping spot patt correct K 38 (40: 42:
44) sts, turn. Work on these sts for left neck
and shoulder. *** Dec 1 st at neck edge on
every row until 32 (34: 36: 38) sts rem. Work
without shaping until Front measures same as
Back to shoulder ending at side edge.
Shape shoulder
Cast off 6 (6: 7: 7) sts at beg of next row.
Work 1 row.
Cast off 6 (7: 7: 7) sts at beg of next row.
Work 1 row.
Cast off 6 (7: 7: 8) sts at beg of next row.
Work 1 row.
Cast off 7 (7: 7: 8) sts at beg of next row.
Work 1 row.
Cast off rem 7 (7: 8: 8) sts.
With right side of work facing slip centre 21
(23: 25: 27) sts to holder. Using 4 mm needles
and with right side facing rejoin yarn to rem sts
and K to end of row. Complete right side
working from *** on left side.

Sleeves

Using $3\frac{1}{4}$ mm needles and B cast on 42 (46: 46: 50) sts.

Work rib as for Back, inc 14 sts evenly across last row.

Change to 4 mm needles.

Work patt as for Back from ** to **.

Cont in st st beg with a K row and using A only, inc 1 st at each end of next and every 8th row until there are 78 (84: 88: 94) sts.

Work without shaping until sleeve measures 40 (40: 42.5: 42.5) cm or 2.5 cm less than required sleeve length.

Using B, K 2 rows.

Using A, work 2 rows st st, beg with a K row.

Using C, K 2 rows.

Using A work 2 rows st st, beg with a K row.

Using B, K 2 rows.

Cast off.

Work 2nd sleeve in same way.

To make up

Press each section on the wrong side under a damp cloth with a warm iron.

Join left shoulder seam.

Collar

Using $3\frac{1}{4}$ mm needles and B and with right side of work facing K across 33 (35: 37: 39) sts from back neck inc 4 sts evenly across sts, pick up and K 17 sts down left side of neck, K 21 (23: 25: 27) sts from centre front inc 4 sts evenly across front, and K up 17 sts up right side of neck. 96 (100: 104: 108) sts.

Work 20 cm K 2, P 2, rib.

Cast off loosely in rib.

Seam collar and right shoulder. Sew in sleeve tops between markers. Seam sides and sleeves. Press seams.

Chapter 8

Lace patterning

There are many different ways of working lace patterns but the majority are constructed by making stitches with the yarn over needle increase and placing decreases both to retain the correct number of stitches and help with the pattern formation.

A simple lace pattern is made by placing a 'yon' next to a K 2 tog, just like a small buttonhole, and repeating this along a row with one or two stitches between each hole. This hole is called an eyelet and can be used in a large number of different ways: dotted about a stocking stitch fabric, placed in vertical lines or grouped in tiny clusters like a flower (figs. 58 and 59).

Fig. 58

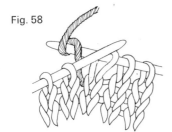

Ridged ribbon eyelet

Cast on an odd number of stitches.
1st row K.
2nd row P.
3rd and 4th rows K.
5th row K 1, * yon, K 2 tog, rep from * to end.
6th row K.

Larger eyelets

Eyelets can be made larger by placing the yarn more than once round the needle point when making the 'yon'. Work to the point two stitches before the eyelet is required, K 2 tog, wind the yarn twice over the needle (abbreviated to y2on) and K 2 tog tbl, then complete the row. On the following row purl to the two strands of yarn over and round the needle, knit into the first loop and purl into the second loop then continue working to the row end.

Fig. 59

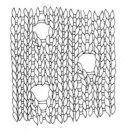

Faggoting

Where a yarn over needle increase and a decrease are worked on every row the fabric is made more lacy and variations introduced by the different arrangement of the yarn over in relation to the decrease.

The simplest of all forms gives a dainty pattern, ideal for stoles and evening wear and is worked by casting on an even number of stitches. The one row pattern is repeated as required.

1st row K 1,* yon, SSK, rep from * to last st, K 1.

Turkish stitch

This basic faggoting becomes Turkish stitch by altering the decrease from an SSK to a K 2 tog. It might be expected that this would make little difference but it is sufficient to alter the appearance (figs. 60 and 61).

Horseshoe lace

The positioning of the eyelets or holes makes a pattern but the position of the decrease also plays its part. Horseshoe lace shows the 'yon' in different positions whilst the decrease is kept in a straight line (fig. 62).

Cast on a number of stitches divisible by 10, plus 1, such as 51 or 71.

1st row P.

2nd row K 1, * yon, K 3, SK2togPO, K 3, yon, K 1, rep from * to end.

3rd row P.

4th row P 1, * K 1, yon, K 2, SK2togPO, K 2, yon, K 1, P 1, rep from * to end.

5th row K 1, * P 9, K 1, rep from * to end.

6th row P 1, * K 2, yon, K 1, SK2togPO, K 1, yon, K 2, P 1, rep from * to end.

7th row K 1, * P 9, K 1, rep from * to end.

8th row P 1, * K 3, yon, SK2togPO, yon, K 3, P 1, rep from * to end.

Repeat rows 1 to 8 as required.

Pinetrees lace

When the decreases are worked similarly to the increase and no longer in a line with each other the pattern changes to become pinetrees lace (fig. 63).

Feather and fan lace

Increases and decreases need not be placed together or even alternate along the row. In feather and fan lace the increases and decreases are worked in groups along the row.

Cast on a number of stitches divisible by 18, such as 54 or 90.

1st row K.

2nd row P.

3rd row *(K 2 tog) 3 times, (yon, K 1) 6 times, (K 2 tog) 3 times, rep from * to end.

4th row K.

Repeat rows 1 to 4 as required (fig. 64).

Fan shell

Increases and decreases do not need to be worked on the same row and fan shell pattern, a

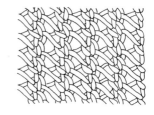

Fig. 60

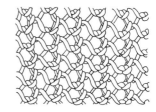

Fig. 61

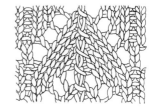

Fig. 62

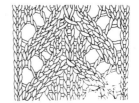

Fig. 63

Fig. 64

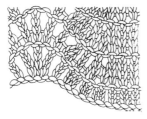

Fig. 65

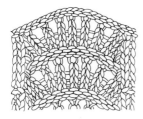

Fig. 66

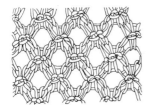

Fig. 67

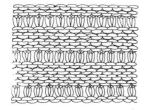

version of feather and fan, delays the increases until the 6th row.

Cast on a number of stitches divisible by 15, plus 4, such as 34 or 64.

1st row P 4, * K 11, P 4, rep from * to end.
2nd row K 4, * P 11, K 4, rep from * to end.
3rd row P 2, * P 2 tog, P 11, P 2 tog tbl, rep from * to last 2 sts, P 2.
4th row K 2, * SSK, K 9, K 2 tog, rep from * to last 2 sts, K 2.
5th row P 2, * P 2 tog, P 7, P 2 tog tbl, rep from * to last 2 sts, P 2.
6th row K 4, * (yon, K 1) 5 times, yon, K 4, rep from * to end.

Repeat rows 1 to 6 as required (fig. 65).

Lace patterns without eyelets

Lace fabrics can also be made without eyelets or made holes. Worked on larger needles than usual some stitches are drawn together to leave more openwork areas around the sides of the grouped stitches.

Open Star Stitch

Cast on a number of stitches divisible by 3, such as 30 or 45.

1st row (wrong side) K 2, * yon, K 3, insert tip of left needle into top of first 3 sts just knitted and lift it over the other 2 sts and off the right needle tip, rep from * to last st, K 1.
2nd row K.
3rd row K 1, * K 3, lift first of 3 knitted sts over other 2 and off right needle, yon, rep from * to last 2 sts, K 2.
4th row K.

Repeat rows 1 to 4 as required (fig. 66).

Lengthening stitches

Stitches which are lengthened are more open than the usual tension and so come under the heading of lace. This can be worked in two ways—

1. By using a very much larger needle for the open row.
2. By winding the yarn more than once round the needle.

Garter stitch worked on 4 mm needles and with double knitting wool takes on a new look when every 8th row only is worked on a 7 or 7½ mm needle (fig. 67).

It is not essential to lengthen all the stitches in a row and many patterns gain a more lacy effect by lengthening only a few. To lengthen a stitch, the yarn is wound round the needle twice instead of once, and the extra loop is dropped when the stitch is worked on the following row. It is the dropping of the loop that allows more yarn to be pulled through the stitch, making it longer. This can be written as yarn twice over (or round) needle and is abbreviated to y2on.

The stitch can be lengthened more by putting the yarn three times over the needle—y3on—or even more times, y4on, y5on. Each time the yarn over needle is worked it forms only one stitch as the other loops are dropped (fig. 68).

Fig. 68

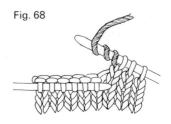

Wave stitch

This stitch uses this technique to make a delightful pattern which is easily worked and grows quickly.

Cast on a number of stitches divisible by 6, plus 1, such as 25 or 76.

1st row K.

2nd row K.

3rd row K 1, * K 1, K 1 y2on, K 1 y3on, K 1 y2on, K 2, rep from * to end.

4th row K 1 st in each stitch, dropping all extra loops.

5th row K.

6th row K.

7th row K 1 y3on, * K 1 y2on, K 3, K 1 y2on, K 1 y3on, rep from * to end.

8th row K 1 st in every stitch, dropping all extra loops.

Repeat rows 1 to 8 as required (fig. 69).

Fig. 69

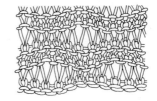

Project: Angel top

This dainty angel top uses a lacy pattern based on garter stitch which allows the edges to be knitted in with the lace and cuts down on making up. A simple design using a four-row repeat, the lace is very easy to work and makes use of a 'yarn over needle' increase and a slipped stitch decrease.

Materials

The yarn used is Patons Fairytale Quickerknit.
5 × 20 g balls.
1 pair each $3\frac{1}{4}$ and $3\frac{3}{4}$ mm needles.
4 small buttons.

Measurements

To fit a 45 cm chest, approx birth to 6 months.
Length to neck, 26 cm.
Sleeve seam, 15 cm.

Tension

Equivalent to 13 sts and 17 rows to 5 cm, measured over st st worked on $3\frac{3}{4}$ mm needles.

Sleeves

Using $3\frac{1}{4}$ mm needles cast on 38 sts.
1st row * K 1, P 1, rep from * to end.
Rep 1st row 9 times.
Next row Rib 2, * M 1, rib 6, rep from * to end (44 sts).
Change to $3\frac{3}{4}$ mm needles and lace pattern.
1st row K.
2nd row K 1, * K 3, yon, sl 1, K 2 tog, psso, yon, rep from * to last st, K 1.
3rd row K.
4th row K 1, * yon, sl 1, K 2 tog, psso, yon, K 3, rep from * to last st, K 1.
Rep last 4 rows 10 times more. Place marker threads at each end of last row.
Rep last 4 rows 5 times more.
Last row K 2 tog, * K 4, K 2 tog, rep from * to end (36 sts).
Leave sts on holder for yoke.
Work a 2nd sleeve in the same way.

Front and Backs (worked in one piece to armholes)

Using $3\frac{3}{4}$ mm needles cast on 176 sts.
K 4 rows.
Begin lace pattern.
1st row K.
2nd row K 4, * K 3, yon, sl 1, K 2 tog, psso, yon, rep from * to last 4 sts, K 4.
3rd row K.
4th row K 4, * yon, sl 1, K 2 tog, psso, yon, K 3, rep from * to last 4 sts, K 4.
Rep last 4 rows 12 times more.
Divide for front and backs.
Next row K 48, leave rem sts on holder until required.
Complete left back on these 48 sts.
Keeping 4 garter st border at centre back work 19 rows more keeping patt correct.
Last row K 4 (K 2 tog) 5 times, * K 2 tog, K 1, rep from * to last 10 sts, (K 2 tog) 5 times (30 sts).
Leave sts on holder for yoke.
With right side of work facing rejoin yarn to rem sts.
Next row K 80, leave rem sts on holder.
Complete front on these sts.
Work 19 rows keeping patt correct.

Last row K 2, * K 2 tog, K 1, rep from * to end.
(54 sts.)
Leave sts on holder for yoke.
With right side of work facing rejoin yarn to last
48 sts and K to end of row.
Work 19 rows keeping patt correct and 4 K st
border at centre back.
Last row (K 2 tog) 5 times, * K 1, K 2 tog, rep
from * to last 14 sts, (K 2 tog) 5 times, K 4.

Yoke
Using $3\frac{1}{4}$ mm needles and with wrong side
facing K 1, K 2 tog, yon, K 27 from right back,
K 36 from 1st sleeve, K 54 from front, K 36 from
2nd sleeve, K 30 from left back.
To work yoke
1st row K 5, K 2 tog, * K 2, K 2 tog, rep to last
7 sts, K 1, K 2 tog, K 4.
K 1 row.
3rd row K 9, * K 2 tog, K 9, rep from * to end.
K 3 rows.
7th row K 9, * K 2 tog, K 8, rep from * to end.
8th row K 1, K 2 tog, yon, K to end.
K 7 rows.
16th row K 1, K 2 tog, yon, K to end.
17th row K 8, * K 2 tog, K 7, rep from * to last
10 sts, K 2 tog, K 8.
K 3 rows.
21st row K 8, * K 2 tog, K 6, rep from * to last
9 sts, K 2 tog, K 7.
K 1 row.
23rd row K 7, * K 2 tog, K 5, rep from * to last
9 sts, K 2 tog, K 7.
24th row K 1, K 2 tog, yon, K to end.
25th row K 7, * K 2 tog, K 4, rep from * to last
8 sts, K 2 tog, K 6.
K 2 rows.
Cast off.
To make up
Join sleeve seams to markers. Seam remaining
part of sleeve to appropriate back and front
section of yoke.
Sew on buttons to correspond with
buttonholes.
Darn in all ends.

Project: Lacy top

Materials
The yarn used is Patons Beehive 4 ply.
3 (4:4:5) 50 g balls.
1 pair each $2\frac{3}{4}$ and $3\frac{1}{4}$ mm needles.

Measurements

To fit 80 (85: 90: 95) cm bust. 32 (34: 36: 38) in bust.

Length from shoulder: Approx 49 (50: 51: 52.5) cm.

Tension

7 sts and 9 rows to 2.5 cm worked on $3\frac{1}{4}$ mm needles.

Front

Using $2\frac{3}{4}$ mm needles cast on 93 (99: 105: 111) sts.

Work 10 cm K 1, P 1 rib beg and ending right side rows with K 1, and finishing with right side facing. Work 1 more row in rib inc 16 sts evenly across row. 109 (115: 121: 127) sts.

Change to $3\frac{1}{4}$ mm needles and pattern.

1st row and all wrong side rows P.

2nd row K 1, * yon, SSK, K 1, K 2 tog, yon, K 1, rep from * to end.

4th row K 1, * yon, K 1, sl 1, K 2 tog, psso, K 1, yon, K 1, rep from * to end.

6th row K 1, * K 2 tog, yon, K 1, yon, SSK, K 1, rep from * to end.

8th row K 2 tog, * (K 1, yon,) twice, K 1, sl 1, K 2 tog, psso, rep from * to last 5 sts, (K 1, yon) twice, K 1, SSK.

Rep rows 1 to 8 until work measures 32.5 cm, ending with a P row.

Shape armholes

Cast off 3 (3: 3: 3) sts at beg of next 4 rows. Keeping patt correct work until front measures 46.25 (47.5: 48.75: 50) cm, ending with a right side row.

Shape neck

1st row P 42, turn and complete first side on these sts.

2nd row Sl 1, patt to end.

3rd row P 38, turn.

4th row Sl 1, patt to end.

5th row P 34, turn.

6th row Sl 1, patt to end.

7th row P 30, turn.

8th row Sl 1, patt to end.

***9th row* P 26, turn.

10th row Sl 1, patt to end.

11th row P 24, turn.

12th row Sl 1, patt to end.

13th row Cast off 7 sts, P 15, turn.

14th row Sl 1, patt to end.

15th row Cast off 7 sts, P 6, turn.

16th row Sl 1, patt to end.

17th row Cast off 6 sts, P across all sts picking

up a loop at point where each turn was made
and purling it together with the next stitch to
avoid leaving holes. **. ·
Work 2nd side thus—
1st row Patt 42, turn.
2nd row Sl 1 purlwise, P to end.
3rd row Patt 38, turn.
4th row Sl 1 purlwise, P to end.
5th row Patt 34, turn.
6th row Sl 1 purlwise, P to end.
7th row Patt 30, turn.
8th row Sl 1 purlwise, P to end.
*** *9th row* Patt 26, turn.
10th row Sl 1 purlwise, P to end.
11th row Patt 24, turn.
12th row Sl 1 purlwise, P to end.
13th row Cast off 7 sts, patt 15, turn.
14th row Sl 1 purlwise, P to end.
15th row Cast off 7 sts, patt 6, turn.
16th row Sl 1 purlwise, P to end.
17th row Cast off 6 sts, K across rem sts
picking up a loop at each turning point and
knitting it together with the next st to avoid
leaving holes.
Change to $2\frac{3}{4}$ mm needles and K 8 rows, dec
1 st at each end of every row.
Cast off. ***.

Back
Work as given for Front to beg of neck shaping.
Work 8 rows more in patt.
Shape neck as given for Front from ** to ** and
complete 2nd side as for Front from *** to ***.
To make up
DO NOT PRESS THIS YARN.
Join shoulder seams and neckband edges.
Using $2\frac{3}{4}$ mm needles and with right side of
work facing pick up and K 88 (96: 106: 114)
sts along armhole edge.
K 6 rows dec 1 st at each end of every row.
Cast off.
Join side and armband seams.

Chapter 9

Using slipped stitches

Without experimenting it may seem surprising that slipped stitches—which are stitches moved from one needle to the other without being worked—can have many uses, but this is not so.

They can be used to help build solid fabric designs and have great potential in patterns using two or more colours, as well as helping a knitted fabric to fold along a vertical line or up the edges of pleats. They can also be used on many other knitted sections to give a neater edge to whatever is being knitted.

Edge stitches

On garments that are to be seamed a slipped stitch at the beginning of each row can help to stop the edges curling and also tightens the edges slightly, making them neater. The neater the edges are, the easier it is to match the stitches and form straight, attractive seams.

On stocking stitch or reversed stocking stitch slip the first stitch purlwise on knit rows and knitwise on purl rows. On garter stitch slip the first stitch purlwise and knit the last stitch on every row.

A chain edge

On garments that are not to be seamed, like scarf edges, an edge of slipped stitches forms a chain of slightly tighter stitches and gives a finish to the edge (fig. 70). On knit rows of stocking stitch slip the first and last stitch knitwise but on purl rows purl every stitch. On rib patterns it will be necessary to begin and end the row with knit stitches so that the first and last stitch can be slipped; on the reverse row, however, the first and last stitches will be purl and should both be worked.

Slipped stitch folds

Slipped stitches can be used to help an edge to fold naturally as might be required for a jacket

Fig. 70

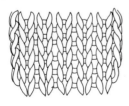

front edging that is to be folded and knitted in with the main sections.

This is done by working to the position of the fold line and slipping the next stitch while keeping the yarn at the back of the work; continue to work to the end of the row. Work the following row in the usual way, working every stitch, and slip the stitch as before on the next and every following alternate row.

This technique is also used on the edge of pleats to make them hang in a fold and can be used at the back and front edges of a pleat.

Single colour patterns

Slipped stitches do not always have to be moved from one needle to the other with the yarn hidden from sight on the wrong side. The yarn can be held across the stitch on the right side of the work as part of the design, the bar formed being used to create pattern.

Slipping stitches means that for that row they are not lengthened, so patterns which used slipped stitches on every alternate row will tend to be closer, tighter fabrics than normal, useful for sportswear, jackets and outdoor garments. When the stitches are slipped on every row the fabric will be very dense and can be worked on thicker needles as required.

Woven stitch

Fig. 71

This stitch carries the yarn across the front of the fabric and resembles a woven texture (fig. 71).
Cast on an even number of stitches.

1st row K 2, * with yf sl 1, K 1, rep from * to end.
2nd row P.
3rd row K 1, * with yf sl 1, K 1, rep from * to last st, K 1.
4th row P.
Repeat rows 1 to 4 as required.

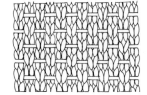

Diagonal and chevron patterns

Fig. 72

These can be made by placing the slipped stitch with the yarn in front so that the bar it forms makes geometric patterns. The bar can also be lengthened and made more noticeable by slipping two or more stitches and carrying the yarn across the front of the group (fig. 72).

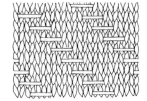

continued on page 75

Opposite *Diagonal Top (pattern on p. 44). A clever effect is achieved using simple increasing and decreasing*

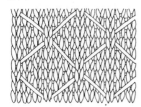

Fig. 73

Quilted lattice

This also uses a slipped stitch whose position is altered on succeeding rows. The effect of this makes a beautiful fabric and one which although easily achieved looks like knitting at its most complex (fig. 73).

Cast on a number of stitches divisible by 6, plus 3, such as 39 or 75.

1st row (wrong side) P.

2nd row K 2, * yf sl 5, K 1, rep from * to last st, K 1.

3rd row P.

4th row K 4, * insert needle under loose strand and K next st, bringing the stitch loop out under the strand, K 5, rep from * ending last rep K 4.

5th row P.

6th row K 1, with yf sl 3, * K 1, yf sl 5, rep from * to last 5 sts, K 1, with yf sl 3, K 1.

7th row P.

8th row K 1, * K next st under loose strand, K 5, rep from * ending last rep K 1.

Repeat rows 1 to 8 as required.

Strengthening sock heels

The yarn across the slipped stitch can also be put to a purpose, rather than just hidden, even when it is used on the wrong side. For example, heels of socks, one of the parts that receive most wear, can be strengthened by working a woven stitch over the surface.

Heel stitch

Cast on an odd number of stitches.

1st row P.

2nd row K 1, * with yb sl 1, K 1, rep from * to end.

Repeat rows 1 and 2 as required.

This can be seen in use on the striped sock, page 54.

Slipped stitches in colour

Slipped stitches have endless uses in colour knitting and can be the source of gay stitch patterns with subtle textures, toned and smooth, easily worked jacquard-type patterns or tweed designs that are worked with only one colour at a time, despite the two- or multi-coloured effect.

Opposite Angel Top in attractive lacy stitch (pattern on p. 66) worn with bootees (pattern on p. 48). Pattern for pink slippers is on p. 50

Brick stitch

This uses the technique of the yarn slipped at the back of the work but carries the main colour up over two rows of the contrast colour. Because the main colour rows are worked in garter stitch (although they can be stocking stitch for a smoother texture), surface interest, colour and pattern are all present (fig. 74).

Cast on a number of stitches divisible by 4, plus 3, such as 27 or 83. The design uses two colours A and B.

1st row Using A, K.

2nd row Using A, K.

3rd row Using B, K 1, * with yb sl 1, K 3, rep from * to last 2 sts, with yb sl 1, K 1.

4th row Using B, P 1, * with yf sl 1, P 3, rep from * to last 2 sts, with yf sl 1, P 1.

5th and 6th rows Using A, K.

7th row Using B, K 3, * with yb sl 1, K 3, rep from * to end.

8th row Using B, P 3, * with yf sl 1, P 3, rep from * to end.

Repeat rows 1 to 8.

Fig. 74

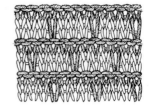

Slipped stitches remain the same length so if slipped over many rows the work around will tend to pucker. This can be used to the advantage of the design by adding another dimension to the fabric as shown in the purled version of blister stitch (fig. 75). Alternatively the slipped stitches can be lengthened by winding the yarn twice or more round the needle and dropping the extra loops on the following row as used for wave stitch, see page 66.

Fig. 75

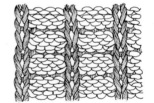

Blister stitch

To work blister stitch cast on a number of stitches divisible by 4, plus 1, such as 25 or 53. Two colours, A and B, are required.

1st row Using A, K.

2nd row Using A, P.

3rd row Using B, K 1, * with yb sl 1, yf, K 3, rep from * to end.

4th row Using B, K 1, * K 2, with yf sl 1, yb, K 1, rep from * to end.

Rep 3rd and 4th rows once.

7th row Using A, K.

8th row Using A, P.

9th row Using B, K 1, * K 2, with yb sl 1, yf, K 1, rep from * to end.

10th row Using B, K 1, * with yf sl 1, yb, K 3, rep from * to end.

Rep 9th and 10th rows once.

Repeat these 12 rows as required.

The duffle coat (see below) uses a very small repeat of slipped stitches to make an interesting tweed which gives scope for using two strongly contrasting colours like navy and cream or two more subtle tones such as a mid-colour and a flecked or marbled yarn of similar tone and thickness. But all slipped stitch patterns need not blend the different rows to this extent.

Swiss check

This pattern shows the possibilities of building up patterns which look like Jacquard or even Fairisle. Using this technique coloured patterns can be knitted without having to use more than one colour at a time as only the stitches that are to be worked in a colour are those worked on that row, other colours being added on other rows. Although this means working four rows to produce two of a jacquard pattern the fact that there is only one colour to use on each row makes up for time lost over working extra rows. For Swiss check pattern cast on a number of stitches divisible by 4, plus 1, such as 25 or 89. Two colours, A and B, are used.

1st row Using A, P.

2nd row Using B, K 1, with yb sl 1, * K 1, with yb sl 3, rep from * to last 3 sts, K 1, with yb sl 1, K 1.

3rd row Using B, K 1, * P 3, with yf sl 1, rep from * to last 4 sts, P 3, K 1.

4th row Using A, K 2, * with yb sl 1, K 3, rep from * to last 3 sts, with yb sl 1, K 2.

5th row Using A, P.

6th row Using B, K 1, * with yb sl 3, K 1, rep from * to end.

7th row Using B, K 1, P 1, * with yf sl 1, P 3, rep from * to last 3 sts, with yf sl 1, P 1, K 1.

8th row Using A, K 4, * with yb sl 1, K 3, rep from * to last st, K 1.

Repeat rows 1 to 8 as required (fig. 76).

Fig. 76

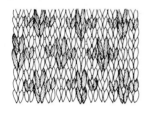

Project: Duffle coat

Slipped stitches make delightful tweeds and the duffle coat is not difficult to work. Firm garter stitch edges add to the style.

Materials

The yarn used is Patons Beehive Double Knitting.

4 (4:5) 50 g balls in main shade, A.

3 (4:4) 50 g balls in contrast, B.

1 pair each 3¼ and 5 mm needles.

6 (8:8) small buttons.

Measurements

To fit a 55 (60: 65) cm, 22 (24: 26) in chest.

Length from shoulder 43.75 (48: 53.25) cm.

Sleeve seam: 21 (26: 30) cm.

Tension

11 sts and 18 rows to 5 cm measured over tweed patt worked on 5 mm needles.

Back

Using 3¼ mm needles and A cast on 75 (81: 87) sts.

K 6 rows.

Change to 5 mm needles and tweed patt.

1st row Using A, K.

2nd row P.

3rd row Using B, K 1, * with yb sl 1, K 1, rep from * to end.

4th row K 1, * with yf sl 1, yb, K 1, rep from * to end.

These 4 rows form the patt and are repeated throughout.

Keeping patt correct work until 30 (33: 37) cm from cast on edge, ending with a 4th row.

Shape armholes

Keeping patt correct cast off 4 sts at beg of next 2 rows. 67 (73: 79) sts.

Work without shaping until armhole measures 13.75 (15: 16.25) cm, ending with a 4th row.

Shape shoulders

Cast off 4 (6: 8) sts at beg of next 2 rows.

Cast off 6 sts at beg of next 6 rows.

Cast off rem 23 (25: 27) sts.

Left front

Using 3¼ mm needles and A, cast on 29 (33: 35) sts.

K 6 rows.

Change to 5 mm needles and work in tweed patt as given for Back until work measures same as Back to armhole, ending at side edge.

Shape armhole

Cast off 4 sts at beg of next row.

Cont without shaping until work measures 5 cm less than back to shoulder ending at centre front edge.

Shape neck

Dec 1 st at neck edge on next and every alt row until 22 (24: 26) sts rem.

Work without shaping until armhole measures same as Back, ending at shoulder edge.

Shape shoulder
Cast off 4 (6:8) sts at beg of next row. Work 1 row.
Cast off 6 sts at beg of next and following 2 alt rows.

Right front
Work as for Left Front noting that shaping is reversed.

Sleeves
Using $3\frac{1}{4}$ mm needles and A, cast on 47 (53: 57) sts.
K 6 rows.
Change to 5 mm needles.
Work in tweed patt as for Back, inc 1 st at each end of 5th and every 8th row until there are 63 (67: 73) sts.
Work without shaping until sleeve measures 21 (26: 30) cm.
Place markers at ends of last row.
Using $3\frac{1}{4}$ mm needles and A, K 6 rows. Cast off.
Work 2nd sleeve in same way.

Front borders
Using $3\frac{1}{4}$ mm needles and A, cast on 17 (19: 19) sts.
K until strip is same length as centre front edge from cast on to start of neck shaping when slightly stretched.
Cast off.
This forms left border for girl and right border for boy. Mark position of buttonholes on strip already worked having last set just below cast off edge at neck.
Work 2nd border in same way, working buttonholes across the row as the markers are reached thus—K 3, yon, K 2 tog, K to last 4 sts, yon, K 2 tog tbl, K 2.
When completed sew border to other front edge.
Sew sleeves into armholes sewing edge of garter stitch border at sleeve top to 4 cast off st edge of armhole.
Join side and sleeve seams.

Hood
Using $3\frac{1}{4}$ mm needles and A, cast on 127 (131:135) sts.
K 6 rows.
Change to 5 mm needles and work in tweed patt as for Back until work measures

12.5 (13.75:15) cm, ending with a 4th row.
Cast off 48 (50:52) sts at beg of next 2 rows.
Cont on rem sts until this section measures same
as cast off side edges.
Cast off.
To make up
DO NOT PRESS THIS GARMENT.
Sew hood to neck edge after seaming cast off
edges to edge of centre strip.
Sew buttons in place to correspond with
buttonholes.

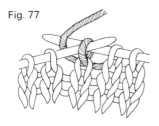

Fig. 77

Chapter 10

Moving and twisting stitches

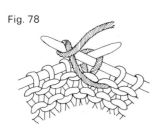

Fig. 78

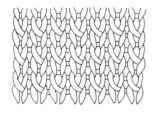

Fig. 79

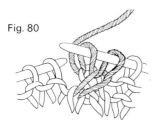

Fig. 80

By giving stitches an extra twist it is possible to alter the smooth surface of stocking stitch to a texture with more movement, very suitable for use with man-made fibres which show the irregularity of tension most knitters find between working knit and purl rows. Stitches can also be twisted together or moved gradually across the surface of the fabric to form lines and diamond patterns.

Single twisted stitches

To knit a stitch through the back of the loop (or tbl) work as for a normal stitch but insert the needle into the back loop instead of the front loop before putting the yarn round the needle tip (fig. 77).

A stitch purled tbl is worked as for a purl stitch but the needle is inserted through the back of the loop (fig. 78). Stocking stitch is renamed Continental stocking stitch when every row of knit stitches is worked tbl and purl rows are purled in the usual way (fig. 79).

Ribs of two stitches can be twisted together to lie either to the right or left without the use of an extra needle but it becomes difficult to twist more than two stitches without using a spare needle.

Twisting two stitches to right

Work to the stitches to be twisted then pass the right needle across the front of the next stitch and with the tip draw the front loop of the next stitch over the passed stitch until there is space to knit it without letting it slip off the needle. Knit the stitch that was passed and slip both stitches off the left needle (fig. 80).

Twisting two stitches to left

Work to the stitches to be twisted and pass the right needle behind the first stitch. Knit the second stitch tbl and without slipping it off the needle knit the first stitch, slipping both stitches off the needle (fig. 81).

Twisted stitch patterns often twist only on

alternate rows but it may be that for a more closed effect twisting is wanted on every row.

On a purl row to twist in the same direction as the right twist pass the needle in front of the first stitch and purl the second stitch, keeping it on the needle until the first stitch has been purled also, then slip both off together.

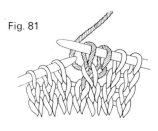

Fig. 81

Similarly, twisting on a purled row to match the left twist, pass the needle behind the first stitch and purl the second stitch through the back of the loop without slipping it off the needle, then purl the first stitch and slip both stitches off the needle together. Stitches are not always twisted the same way but may be altered to give the rib a more winged effect (fig. 82).

Stitches can be moved across the fabric in this way, the stitch which is to show the move being worked as a knit stitch standing out against a purled background. For this the stitches would be moved in the same way as described but either the first or second stitch would be purled instead of knitted to take its place in the background (fig. 83).

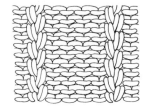

Fig. 82

Cabling

When moving larger groups of stitches around themselves like a rope or cable or across the fabric it is easier not to twist them but to slip them onto a small cable needle and hold them at the back or the front of the work as directed in the instructions while other stitches are knitted into their place. The slipped stitches can then take their new position in the row.

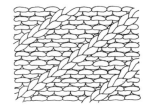

Fig. 83

To the beginner cable patterns look immensely complex but in fact are no more difficult than knitting and purling ordinary stitches and should always be attempted.

A cable of six stitches which crosses to the right and is on a purled background would be worked thus—

1st row Purl to the 6 sts for the cable, K 6, P to the end.

2nd row K to 6 cable sts, P 6, K to end.

Rep 1st and 2nd rows once.

5th row P to 6 cable sts, slip the first 3 sts onto a small cable needle and hold at back of work, K the next 3 sts, then K the 3 sts from the cable needle, P to end of row.

Fig. 84

6th row Work as the 2nd row.

7th and 8th rows Work as 1st and 2nd rows.

Repeat these 8 rows and the rope or cable will begin to be visible (fig. 84).

To work a cable turning left the first 3 sts when

82

Fig. 85

Fig. 86

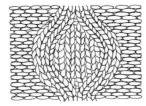

slipped onto the cable needle are held in front of the work, the next 3 sts are knitted and then the 3 sts from the cable needle (fig. 85).

The cabled stitches might have been abbreviated to read cable 6 right or C6R and cable 6 left or C6L. In some designs front might have been used instead of the direction left and back instead of the direction right, the abbreviation becoming C6F or C6B.

The variety of cable patterns is so great with differences in width, some being purled, others knitted and the cabling turning left or right, that individual abbreviations with full explanations are usually given with any instructions. See the pattern for the zipper jacket on page 84.

Right and left turning cables may be alternated to form larger cables. A rounded cable is formed by placing two cables of 6 stitches together and the instructions use C6B and C6F as previously explained.

Round cable
Cast on 18 sts.
1st row P 3, K 12, P 3.
2nd row K 3, P 12, K 3.
Rep 1st and 2nd rows once.
5th row P 3, C6B, C6F, P 3.
6th row K 3, P 12, K 3.
Rep 1st and 2nd rows twice.
11th row P 3, C6F, C6B, P 3.
12th row As 2nd.
Repeat as required (fig. 86).
Cable patterns are very often worked in panels, often teamed with twisted stitches, but they can also be used as all-over fabrics.

Arrow cable
This uses stitches which travel across the fabric as well as cables to form an interesting and purposeful pattern.
The abbreviations used are—
C4B—slip 2 sts onto cable needle and hold at back of work, K next 2 sts, K 2 sts from cable needle.
C2F— slip next st to cable needle and hold in front, P next st, then K st from cable needle.
C2B—slip next st to cable needle and hold at back, K 1, then P st from cable needle.
Cast on a number of sts divisible by 16, plus 4, such as 36 or 84.
1st row P 4, * P 1, K 3, P 4, K 3, P 5, rep from * to end.
2nd row K 4, * C2F, P 2, K 4, P 2, C2B, K 4, rep from * to end.

3rd row K all K sts and P all P sts.
4th row C4B, * P 1, C2F, P 1, C4B, P 1, C2B,
P 1, C4B, rep from * to end.
5th row K all K sts and P all P sts.
6th row K 4, * P 2, C2F, K 4, C2B, P 2, K 4, rep
from * to end.
7th row K all K sts and P all P sts.
8th row C4B, * P 4, C4B, rep from * to end.
Rep rows 1 to 8 as required.

Project: Zipper jacket

First attempts at cabling and moving stitches are
best undertaken on a jacket where the pattern is
only used on a small area and the back and
sleeves are worked plain. This jacket has a neat
zip and the pattern takes pride of place on the
fronts only, where it contrasts with the reversed
stocking stitch fabric.

Read the special abbreviations before beginning to knit so that no mistakes are made.

Materials
The yarn used is Patons Capstan.
12 (13:14:15) 50 g balls.
1 pair each $3\frac{1}{4}$ and 4 mm needles.
1 open-end zipper 55 cm (22 in) long.

Measurements
To fit an 80 (85:90:95) cm, 32 (34:36:38) in
bust/chest.
Length to shoulder: 62.5 (62.5:65:65) cm.
Sleeve seam: 40 (42:44:45) cm.

Tension
10 sts and 13 rows to 5 cm, measured over
reversed stocking st worked on 4 mm needles.

Abbreviations
C5 – Slip next 3 sts to cable needle and hold
    at front, K next 2 sts, slip last of 3 sts
    from cable needle to left needle and P it,
    K rem 2 sts from cable needle.
C3R – Slip next st to cable needle and hold at
    back, K next 2 sts, P 1 st from cable
    needle.
C3L – Slip next 2 sts to cable needle and hold
    at front, P next st, K 2 sts from cable
    needle.

The pattern panel
The panel is worked over 21 sts.
1st row P 8, K 2, P 1, K 2, P 8.
2nd row K 8, P 2, K 1, P 2, K 8.
3rd row P 8, K 2, P 1, K 2, P 8.

4th row K 8, P 2, K 1, P 2, K 8.
5th row P 8, C5, P 8.
6th row K 8, P 2, K 1, P 2, K 8.
Rep rows 1 to 6 once more.
13th row P 7, C3R, P 1, C3L, P 7.
14th row K 7, P 2, K 3, P 2, K 7.
15th row P 6, C3R, P 3, C3L, P 6.
16th row K 6, P 2, K 5, P 2, K 6.
17th row P 5, C3R, P 5, C3L, P 5.
18th row K 5, P 2, K 7, P 2, K 5.
19th row P 4, C3R, P 7, C3L, P 4.
20th row K 4, P 2, K 9, P 2, K 4.
21st row P 3, C3R, P 9, C3L, P 3.
22nd row K 3, P 2, K 11, P 2, K 3.
23rd row P 2, C3R, P 11, C3L, P 2.
24th row K 2, P 2, K 13, P 2, K 2.
25th row P 1, C3R, P 13, C3L, P 1.
26th row K 1, P 2, K 15, P 2, K 1.
27th row P 1, C3L, P 13, C3R, P 1.
28th row K 2, P 2, K 13, P 2, K 2.
29th row P 2, C3L, P 11, C3R, P 2.
30th row K 3, P 2, K 11, P 2, K 3.
31st row P 3, C3L, P 9, C3R, P 3.
32nd row K 4, P 2, K 9, P 2, K 4.
33rd row P 4, C3L, P 7, C3R, P 4.
34th row K 5, P 2, K 7, P 2, K 5.
35th row P 5, C3L, P 5, C3R, P 5.
36th row K 6, P 2, K 5, P 2, K 6.
37th row P 6, C3L, P 3, C3R, P 6.
38th row K 7, P 2, K 3, P 2, K 7.
39th row P 7, C3L, P 1, C3R, P 7.
40th row K 8, P 2, K 1, P 2, K 8.
Rep 5th and 6th rows once, then rows 1 to 6 once.
Rep rows 13 to 40 once, then 5th and 6th rows once.
Cont working rows 1 to 6 to shoulder cast off, on last row dec 1 st on each of 2 cable ridge sts.

Back
Using $3\frac{1}{4}$ mm needles cast on 79 (85: 89: 95) sts.
** *1st row* P 1, * K 1, P 1, rep from * to end.
2nd row K 1, * P 1, K 1, rep from * to end.
Rep 1st and 2nd rows 10 times then 1st row once. **.
Work 2nd row inc 6 (5: 6: 5) times evenly across row. 85 (90: 95: 100) sts.
Change to 4 mm needles and work in reversed st st beg with a P row. (P 1 row, K 1 row repeated.)
Cont until work measures 41.25 (41.25: 40: 40) cm, ending with a K row.

Shape armholes

Cast off 4 (4: 5: 5) sts at beg of next 2 rows,
then dec 1 st at each end of next and every alt
row until 65 (68: 73: 76) sts rem.
Work without shaping until Back measures
60 (60: 60: 60) cm, ending with a K row.

Shape shoulders

Cast off 7 (7: 7: 7) sts at beg of next 2 rows.
Cast off 6 (6: 7: 7) sts at beg of next 2 rows.
Cast off 6 (6: 7: 7) at beg of next 2 rows.
Cast off 27 (30: 31: 34) sts.

Sleeves

Using 3 mm needles cast on 41 (43: 45: 47)
sts.
Work as for Back from ** to **.
Work 1 row more in rib inc evenly 3 sts across
row.
44 (46: 48: 50) sts.
Change to 4 mm needles and work in reversed
st st beg with a P row, inc 1 st at each end of
5th and every foll 8th row until there are 68
(68: 72: 72) sts.
Work without shaping until sleeve measures
40 (42: 44: 45) cm or required sleeve length,
ending with a K row.

Shape top

Cast off 4 (4: 5: 5) sts at beg of next 2 rows.
Dec 1 st at each end of next and every alt row
until 38 (38: 40: 40) sts rem. K 1 row.
Dec 1 st at each end of every row until 16 (16:
18: 18) sts rem.
Cast off 2 (2: 3: 3) sts at beg of next 2 rows.
Work on rem 12 sts until this strip is the same
length as cast off shoulder edge when slightly
stretched. Cast off.
Work second sleeve in same way.

Left front

Using 3¼ mm needles cast on 39 (43: 45: 47)
sts.
Work as for Back from ** to **.
Work inc row thus—
1st size Rib 9, M 1, rib 10, M 1, rib 1, M 1,
rib 13, M 1, rib 6. (43 sts).
2nd size Rib 20, M 1, rib 1, M 1, rib 12, M 1,
rib 10. (46 sts).
3rd size Rib 9, M 1, rib 11, M 1, rib 1, M 1,
rib 10, M 1, rib 14. (49 sts).
4th size Rib 6, M 1, rib 5, M 1, rib 9, M 1, rib 1,
M 1, rib 10, M 1, rib 16. (52 sts).

For all sizes

1st row P 10 (11: 12: 13), work panel over

next 21 sts, P to end.

2nd row K 12 (14: 16: 18), work 2nd row of panel over 21 sts, K to end.

Cont working panel with reversed st st at either side until work measures same as Back to armhole ending at side edge.

Shape armhole

Keeping panel patt correct cast off 4 (4: 5: 5) sts at beg of next row. Work 1 row.

Dec 1 st at beg of next and every alt row until 33 (35: 38: 40) sts rem.

Work without shaping until front measures 55 (55: 55: 55) cm, ending at centre front edge.

Shape neck

Cast off 7 (8: 9: 10) sts, work to end.

Dec 1 st at neck edge on every row until 21 (21: 23: 23) sts rem. This is 2 sts more than required for shoulder, each cable panel of 2 sts is dec on last row before cast off edge is worked.

Work without shaping until armhole measures same as Back to shoulder edge.

Shape shoulder

Cast off 7 (7: 7: 7) sts at beg of next row. Work 1 row.

Cast off 6 (6: 7: 7) sts at beg of next row. Work 1 row.

Cast off 6 (6: 7: 7) sts at beg of next row.

Right front

Work as for Left front reversing patt.

Increase row is worked thus—

1st size Rib 6, M 1, rib 13, M 1, rib 1, M 1, rib 10, M 1, rib 9.

2nd size Rib 10, M 1, rib 12, M 1, rib 1, M 1, rib 20.

3rd size Rib 14, M 1, rib 10, M 1, rib 1, M 1, rib 11, M 1, rib 9.

4th size Rib 16, M 1, rib 10, M 1, rib 1, M 1, rib 9, M 1, rib 5, M 1, rib 6.

1st row P 12 (14: 16: 18), work 21 panel sts, P to end.

2nd row K 10 (11: 12: 13), work 21 panel sts, K to end.

Complete as for other side.

To make up

Press all sections under a damp cloth with a warm iron.

Join shoulder straps on sleeves to cast off shoulder edges.

Sew in sleeves. Join side and sleeve seams.

Sew in zip.

Neckband

Using 3¼mm needles and with right side facing K up 20 (21 : 22 : 23) sts up right side of neck, K up 9 (9:9:9) sts from saddle, K 27 (31 : 31 : 35) sts from centre back inc 1 st at centre on 2nd and 4th sizes, K up 9 (9:9:9) sts from other saddle and 20 (21 : 22 : 23) sts down left front neck.
85 (91 : 93 : 99) sts.
Work 20 rows K 1, P 1 rib beg with a P st.
Fold neckband in half to wrong side and slip st in place.
Press seams.

Chapter 11

Adaptations

Adapting an existing pattern has limitations but for the knitter prepared to stay within these there are many ways in which individuality can be brought to basic designs, without losing the safety of tried shaping and stitch numbers correctly sized for the garment.

Adapting a design does not mean taking a garment in double knitting with set-in sleeves and a stocking stitch pattern and using it to make a raglan-sleeved, 4-ply garment in garter stitch. This is designing; and for this many calculations are required which are certainly outside the scope of adaptation.

An adaptation must use the basic design, retaining the original tension, but can add small changes such as the shape of the neckline, the length, the colour, as well as texture and pattern variations.

Points to avoid

Avoid changes in tension through use of a yarn that will not knit to the same tension or a stitch pattern which alters either the number of stitches or rows to the given measurement. Always make a tension swatch to check that the tension is the same as that specified for the original garment, altering the needle size if necessary.

Avoid altering sleeve seam shaping. Such alterations require working out on graph paper with some knowledge of what altering involves.

Avoid changes in length if the basic garment has a lot of shaping. Coats, jackets and sweaters which are basically straight sided or nearly so can be lengthened or shortened provided care is taken.

Changing length

Remember when making an alteration to the length, whether it is to be shortened or lengthened, that the amount of yarn will be affected.

When planning to lengthen a garment make sure that you have extra yarn of the same dye lot.

Length changes are most easily made on instructions that work to a stated measurement rather than instructions which give the number of rows or patterns to work. Where rows or patterns are used as a measurement it will be essential to make a swatch before starting the garment to find the number of rows required to be added or subtracted from the original instructions to obtain the new measurement. The time taken to make the swatch is not lost for without it work will perhaps result in a reknit whereas with the exact measurement work can be carried out without any doubts.

Avoid making alterations which will reduce numbers of increases or decreases. If rows are to be subtracted over shaped areas work out the number of rows and subtract these from between several shapings so that there is no sudden alteration at any one point.

Length to be added to sleeves should be added at the top and not at the cuff where it might cause the upper part of the sleeve to be too tight.

Changing necklines

Necklines can be altered if planned on graph paper. Round, V or square necks can be replaced by one of the others but it is best to retain the back neck as written as this sets the width of the front neck and it is not difficult to plan out a new shape on paper with this knowledge.

Stripes

Stripes are the simplest way of adapting any pattern and can give great variety. Narrow stripes may be all that is required but wide or varied stripes or vertical bands of colour can be most dramatic.

Using the vertical stripe technique for colour joins (page 52), blocks and geometric shapes also make for unusual effects and colour combinations. Pre-plan on graph paper to see what the finished result will be like.

Narrow stripes were added to one version of the V-necked sweater given as a project at the end of this chapter.

continued on page 93

Opposite *Colourful Striped Socks (pattern on p. 54)*

Pattern panels

Panels introduced into a garment allow the use of interesting patterns which might prove difficult to adapt to shaping. Narrow panels of cable or lace will alter the tension so slightly that it will be safe to use them. Because of shaping panels should be stopped short of necklines or raglan shaping unless it is quite obvious that it will be oasy to handle (see lace-panelled version of the V-necked sweater at the end of this chapter).

Lace pattern can be worked all over a basic design, provided that it is not too open and does not therefore alter the tension. This can be avoided by working on a size smaller needle so reducing width gained by openness. It is best to work a swatch to make certain that a needle change is sufficient.

Panels and borders of textured surfaces such as those in Chapter 3 can give interest and add light and shade even without a colour change, and might be used inside a garter stitch edge to give the appearance of a yoke on an otherwise plain sweater.

Decorative band or welt

Colour can also be added in small quantities by banding cuffs and welts with Fairisle designs or small Jacquard patterns. The smallest V-necked sweater makes use of a slipped stitch pattern to give both colour and texture to sleeve and body (see V-necked sweater with decorative border at the end of this chapter).

When placing bands and borders work a few rows of background stitch above ribbed welts before starting the pattern for maximum effect.

Project: Basic V-necked sweater

This pattern is for a basic sweater, which can be given many different looks by the addition of other colours, texture or stitch, all without altering the basic tension or redesigning any part of it.

Materials

The yarn used is Patons Double Knitting Wool.
5 (6: 7: 8: 8: 9: 9: 10: 11) 50 g balls.
1 pair each $3\frac{1}{4}$ and 4 mm needles.

Opposite *Lacy Top in delicate 4-ply yarn (pattern on p. 68)*

Measurements

To fit 65 (70: 75: 80: 85: 90: 95: 100: 105) cm
26 (28: 30: 32: 34: 36: 38: 40: 42) in bust.
Length from shoulder: 41 (44: 48: 54: 56: 57:
63: 65: 66) cm.
Sleeve seam: 30 (34: 38: 42: 43: 43: 44: 46:
46) cm.

Tension

11 sts and 15 rows to 5 cm, measured over
stocking stitch worked on 4 mm needles.

Back

Using 3¼ mm needles cast on 70 (76: 82: 84:
90: 96: 100: 106: 112) sts.
1st row * K 1, P 1, rep from * to end.
Rep 1st row until rib measures 5 (5: 5: 7.5: 7.5:
7.5: 7.5: 7.5: 7.5) cm, ending with a right side
row.
Next row Rib 7 (8: 8: 7: 6: 6: 8: 7: 7), M 1, *
rib 11 (12: 13: 10: 11: 12: 12: 13: 14), M 1,
rep from * to last 8 (8: 9: 7: 7: 6: 8: 8: 7) sts,
rib to end.
Change to 4 mm needles and cont in st st, beg
with a K row.
Work until 24 (26.5: 29: 34: 34: 34: 37.5:
37.5: 37.5) cm from cast on edge, or required
length to raglan, ending with a P row.

Shape raglans

Cast off 3 (3: 3: 4: 4: 4: 4: 4: 4) sts at beg of
next 2 rows.
Work 2 rows without shaping.
Next row K 2, K 2 tog tbl, K to last 4 sts, K 2
tog, K 2.
Work 3 rows without shaping.
4th, 5th, 6th, 7th, 8th, and 9th sizes Rep last
4 rows (2: 2: 2: 4: 4: 4) times more.
All sizes
Next row K 2, K 2 tog tbl, K to last 4 sts, K 2
tog, K 2.
Next row P.
Rep last 2 rows until 24 (26: 28: 30: 32: 34:
36: 38: 40) sts rem, ending with a P row.
Leave rem sts on holder until required for
neckband.

Front

Work as for Back until 4 rows less than Back to
raglan shaping.

Divide for neck

1st row K 35 (38: 41: 43: 46: 49: 51: 54: 57)
sts, K 2 tog, K 1.
Leave rem sts on holder for other side.

2nd row P.

3rd row K.

4th row P.

5th row Cast off 3 (3: 3: 4: 4: 4: 4: 4: 4) sts, work to last 3 sts, K 2 tog, K 1.

Cont working raglan as for Back. AT SAME TIME dec at centre front on every 5th (5th: 5th: 4th: 4th: 4th: 4th: 4th: 4th) row until 8 (8: 8: 8: 8: 8: 9: 9: 9) sts rem.

Cont dec 1 st at raglan edge on every alt row as before, keeping neck edge straight until 3 sts rem.

Next row K 3 tog. Cut yarn and draw through last st.

With right side of work facing rejoin yarn to rem sts.

1st row K 1, K 2 tog tbl, K to last 4 sts, K 2 tog, K 2.

Complete to correspond with other side.

Sleeves

Using 3¼ mm needles cast on 36 (38: 40: 40: 42: 44: 46: 48: 50) sts. Work in rib as for Back, ending with a right side row.

Next row Rib 4 (5: 5: 5: 3: 4: 5: 4: 5), M 1, * rib 9 (9: 10: 6: 7: 7: 7: 8: 8), M 1, rep from * to last 5 (6: 5: 5: 4: 5: 6: 4: 5) sts, rib to end.

Change to 4 mm needles and st st beg with a K row and inc 1 st at each end of 5th (3rd: 5th: 3rd: 5th: 5th: 5th: next: next) and every foll 8th (8th: 9th: 10th: 9th: 8th: 7th: 7th: 7th) row until there are 56 (60: 64: 66: 70: 74: 80: 84: 86) sts.

Work without shaping until sleeve measures 30 (34: 38: 42: 43: 43: 44: 46: 46) cm, or required length, ending with a P row.

Shape raglans

Cast off 3 (3: 3: 4: 4: 4: 4: 4: 4) sts at beg of next 2 rows.

Work 2 rows without shaping.

Next row K 2, K 2 tog tbl, K to last 4 sts, K 2 tog, K 2.

Work 3 rows without shaping.

4th, 5th, 6th, 7th, 8th and 9th sizes

Rep last 4 rows (2: 3: 3: 3: 3: 4) times more.

All sizes

Next row K 2, K 2 tog tbl, K to last 4 sts, K 2 tog, K 2.

Next row P.

Rep last 2 rows until 8 sts rem, ending with a P row.

Next row K 2, K 2 tog tbl, K 2 tog, K 2.

Leave rem sts on holder for neckband.

Neckband

Block and press each section under a damp cloth with a warm iron.

Join raglan seams using an invisible seam with the exception of the left back seam.

Using $3\frac{1}{4}$ mm needles and with right side of work facing K up 6 sts from top of 1st sleeve, K up 40 (44: 48: 52: 56: 60: 64: 68: 72) sts from left front neck, K up 40 (44: 48: 52: 56: 60: 64: 68: 72) sts from other side of neck, K 6 sts from top of 2nd sleeve and K 24 (26: 28: 30: 32: 34: 36: 38: 40) from back neck.

1st row * P 1, K 1, rep from * to 2 sts before centre front, P 2 tog, P 2 tog tbl, K 1, P 1, rep from * to end.

2nd row Rib to 2 sts before centre, K 2 tog tbl, K 2 tog, rib to end.

Rep last 2 rows twice more.

Cast off.

To finish making up

Seam neckband and raglan.

Seam sleeves and side seams.

Press seams.

Striped version

Narrow stripes were added to the sweater still using the smooth side of the stocking stitch as the right side. The fabric could have been reversed using the rougher surface as the right side, creating a feature of the looped join between one colour and another.

Decorative border

Both texture and colour are added in a decorative border by the use of a simple slipped stitch design which has only one colour worked on any one row.

The pattern rows are worked as follows—

1st row Using main colour, K.

2nd row Using main colour, P.

3rd row Using 1st contrast, K.

4th row Using 1st contrast, K.

5th row Using 2nd contrast, K 1, * with yb sl 1, K 1, rep from * to end.

6th row Using 2nd contrast, K 1, * with yf sl 1, yb, K 1, rep from * to end.

7th row Using 1st contrast, K.

8th row Using 1st contrast, K.

Repeat these 8 rows twice.

For the larger sizes this pattern repeat might be too narrow and a third repeat could be added.

N.B. The pattern does not use the same number of stitches as the basic design but requires the addition of one extra stitch. This stitch is added at the transition from ribbing to stocking stitch and can be decreased again at the end of the border rows.

As one stitch does little to alter the size it can also be carried up the sweater and used as a central stitch in the V neck.

Lace-panelled version
In this sweater the panels were added only to the front giving the pattern interest but not adding vastly to the amount of work involved. The lace panels were kept within a controlled measurement and not allowed to reach into areas where neck or raglan shaping might have proved difficult.

Cable panels or patterns using travelling stitches or twisted stitches can be also used in this way and can also be used to decorate the sleeve.

The lace panel is worked over 9 stitches.

1st row P.

2nd row K 3, yon, sl 2 knitwise, K 1, p2sso, yon, K 3.

3rd row P.

4th row K 2, SSK, yon, K 1, yon, K 2 tog, K 2.

5th row P.

6th row K 1, SSK, yon, sl 2 knitwise, K 1, p2sso, yon, K 2 tog, K 1.

7th row P 2, purl into front and back of next yon, P 1, purl into front and back of next yon, P 2.

8th row (SSK, yon,) twice, K 1, (yon, K 2 tog,) twice.

These 8 rows were repeated for the length of the lace panel required.

Chapter 12

Some interesting techniques

In knitting many stitches, for example cable patterns, look exceedingly complicated if they have never been attempted, but in fact can be very simple to work.

Because all stitches can only be treated in one of three ways—knitted or purled or left unworked—beginners should never feel that they are not able to work cables or bobble patterns, that looped fabrics are beyond them and that dropped stitch patterns or smocked designs sound terrifying. In order to do such patterns all that is required is that the instructions should be read carefully before they are tried out.

Bobbles

Bobbles are worked on one row and usually completed on that same row before the remainder of the stitches in the row are worked. However, small bobbles (which are really called popcorns) are more likely to be made on one row and completed on the next.

Making a bobble

Work to the position where the bobble is required. Make 5 stitches out of the next stitch thus (K 1, yon, K 1, yon, K 1 all into the next st) turn and purl 5 sts, turn and knit 5 sts, turn, P 2 tog, P 1, P 2 tog, turn, K 3 tog. This completes the bobble and you then continue working to the row end, adding in more bobbles if required. (Figs. 87 and 88.)

Bobbles can be worked as stocking stitch on a purled background or a purled bobble may be placed against a stocking stitch panel. The choice is determined by the remainder of the design.

Popcorn bobbles

Work to required position. Make 5 sts out of the next stitch by knitting into the front, back, front, back and front of the stitch and then complete the row. On the following row work to the five

Fig. 87

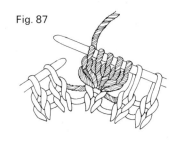

Fig. 88

Fig. 89

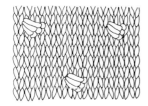

made stitches and reduce them to one by working K 5 tog tbl (fig. 89).

Bobbles and popcorns can be arranged to accentuate other patterns, to complement cables or used on their own as all over textures or in panels.

Loop stitch

Sooner or later every knitter may find it useful to know how to do this stitch which produces a fur-like fabric. It can be effective for a lion's mane or a fluffy bonnet for a baby, it could be used on a bolero or waistcoat, collars and cuffs, or for knitting fringed edges.

Cast on an odd number of stitches.

1st row K.

2nd row * K 1, insert needle into next stitch and place left forefinger behind the needle tip so that the yarn can be wound round the finger and needle together, repeat the winding process twice (fig. 90) then draw the loops through the stitch, slip them back to the left needle and knit tog as 1 st (fig. 91), rep from * to last st, K 1.

The loop-making row may be repeated after one row or three and the position should be alternated so that a loop is made over a knit stitch on the last row.

Fig. 90

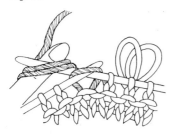

Fig. 91

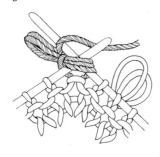

Dropped stitch patterns

Dropped stitches are experienced by every knitter but some stitches are dropped on purpose to form clusters of stitches.

Cast on a number of stitches divisible by 3, plus 2, such as 32 or 71.

1st, 3rd and 5th rows K 2, * P 1, K 2, rep from * to end.

2nd and 4th rows P 2, * K 1, P 2, rep from * to end.

6th row P 2, * drop next st off needle and unravel it 4 rows down so that there are 4 loose strands behind st, insert the right needle tip from front into fifth stitch down and also under the 4 strands and knit it catching the strands behind it and drawing it up, P 2, rep from * to end.

Repeat rows 1 to 6 as required (fig. 92).

Clustered stitches

Stitches can be tied or have the yarn wound round them after working to form flat bobbles or to give the appearance of two ribs tied together as smocking might do in embroidery.

Fig. 92

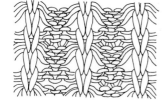

After knitting the stitches to be tied, slip them onto a cable needle and bring the yarn round below the needle across the front and round to the back. Wind the yarn several times round and then slip the stitches onto the right needle and continue to work along the row. (Fig. 93.)

Banded rib

This uses another method of adding horizontal strands to a vertical rib (fig. 94).

Cast on a number of stitches divisible by 4, such as 24 or 68.

1st and 3rd rows K 1, * P 2, K 2, rep from * to last 3 sts, P 2, K 1.

2nd row P 1, K 1, * skip next 3 sts and insert needle into front of 4th st and draw through a loop, then K 1st st on left needle, P next 2 sts on left needle and drop 4th st which has already been knitted off needle, rep from * to last 2 sts, K 1, P 1.

4th row P 1, * K 2, P 2, rep from * ending K 2, P 1.

Repeat rows 1 to 4.

Brioche stitches

Fisherman's rib introduces a new family of stitches which have many uses and are called Brioche stitches. Knitted in fine yarns they can give light, almost fluffy textures but in thicker yarns they are ideal for sportswear and jackets. Fisherman's rib is reversible and although it uses a lot of yarn it is worth any extra effort.

Cast on an even number of stitches.

1st row (preparation row only) K 2, * P 1, K 1, rep from * to end.

2nd row Sl 1 knitwise, * K into the next st inserting the needle into the loop below the stitch and slip this and the stitch above off the left needle (abbreviation K 1b), P 1, rep from * to last st, K 1.

Rep this 2nd row throughout (fig. 95).

The jacket on page 122 is worked in an economical version of this rib in which the knit stitches are worked only on alternate rows, thus using less yarn.

Fig. 93

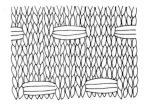

Fig. 94

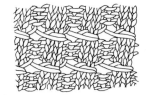

Fig. 95

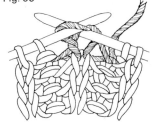

Project: Lion

A looped mane makes the lion additionally cuddly but it can be worked by ordinary fringing if knitted loops prove difficult. Chapter 12 gives advice on how to work and although so effective there is no complex technique to master.

Materials

The yarn used is Patons Trident Double Knitting.

4 × 25 g balls in main shade, A.

2 × 25 g balls in contrast, B.

1 pair $5\frac{1}{2}$ mm needles.

Stuffing.

Small scraps of felt and embroidery cotton for face.

Measurements

Approx 25 cm tall when complete.

Tension

8 sts to 5 cm measured over st st worked on $5\frac{1}{2}$ mm needles.

Special note

Two strands of yarn are used together for each section of the lion.

Front legs

Using 2 strands of A and $5\frac{1}{2}$ mm needles cast on 19 sts.

Work in st st beg with a K row.

Work 4 rows.

5th row K 4, (K 2 tog) twice, K 3, (SSK) twice, K 4.

6th row P 3, (P 2 tog) twice, P 1, (P 2 tog) twice, P 3.

Work 6 rows.

13th row K 1, M 1, K 4, M 1, K 1, M 1, K 4, M 1, K 1. (15 sts).

Work 5 rows.

19th row K 1, M 1, K to last st, M 1, K 1.

Work 3 rows.

23rd row K 1, M 1, K to last st, M 1, K 1.

P 1 row.

Cast off 9 sts. K to end of row and leave rem 10 sts on holder.

Work 2nd leg in same way omitting last P row and working cast off row on P row to reverse shaping.

Body

Using 2 strands of A and $5\frac{1}{2}$ mm needles cast on 44 sts.

Work in st st, beg with a K row.

Work 7 rows.

Cast off 12 sts at beg of next 2 rows for back legs.

Work 3 rows.

Inc 1 st at each end of next and foll 2 alt rows.

P 1 row.

Next row K 1, M 1, K 9, K 2 tog, K 2, SSK, K 9, M 1, K 1. (26 sts).

P 1 row.

Rep last 2 rows twice. Cut yarn.

Join in front legs

With right side of work facing K 10 sts from top of 1st leg, K 26 sts across body and K 10 sts from top of 2nd leg.

P 1 row.

Next row K 18, (K 2 tog) twice, K 2, (SSK) twice, K 18.

P 1 row.

Next row K 1, M 1, K 17, K 2 tog, K 2, SSK, K 17, M 1, K 1.

P 1 row.

Next row K 18, K 2 tog, K 2, SSK, K 18.

P 1 row.

Next row K 1, M 1, K 16, K 2 tog, K 2, SSK, K 16, M 1, K 1.

P 1 row.

Next row K 15, (K 2 tog,) twice, K 2, (SSK,) twice, K 15.

P 1 row.

Next row K 1, SSK, K 10, (K 2 tog) twice, K 2, (SSK) twice, K 10, K 2 tog, K 1.

P 1 row.

Next row K 1, SSK, K 7, (K 2 tog) twice, K 2, (SSK) twice, K 7, K 2 tog, K 1.

P 1 row.

Next row K 7, (K 2 tog) twice, K 2, (SSK) twice, K 7.

P 1 row.

Divide for head and face

1st row K 1, M 1, K 6, K 2 tog, K 1, turn.

Work right side of face on these sts, leaving other sts on holder or spare needle.

2nd row P 9, M 1, K 1, turn, cast on 4 sts.

3rd row K 12, K 2 tog, K 1.

P 1 row.

5th row (K 1, M 1,) 6 times, K 5, K 2 tog, K 1.

P 1 row.

7th row K 4, (M 1, K 1,) twice, K 10, K 2 tog, K 1.

P 1 row.

9th row K 17, K 2 tog, K 1. Place marker thread at beg of this row.

P 1 row.

11th row K 1, SSK, K to last 3 sts, K 2 tog, K 1.

P 1 row.

Rep last 2 rows twice more.

Work 4 rows.

Cast off 3 sts at beg of next 2 rows.

Cast off rem sts.

With right side of work facing rejoin yarn to rem sts and work other side of head to correspond with first side, reversing shaping.

To reverse shaping read rows from end to beg
or rejoin yarn with wrong side of work facing
and read K for P and P for K.

Front gusset

Using 2 strands of A and 5½mm needles
cast on 6 sts.
Work in st st beg with a K row.
Inc 1 st at each end of every K row until there
are 16 sts.
Place marker threads at end of last row.
Work 8 rows and place marker threads on last
row.
Work 3 rows more.
Next row K 4, (K 2 tog) twice, K 2, (SSK)
twice, K 4.
Work 3 rows.
Next row K 3, K 2 tog, K 2, SSK, K 3.
Work 3 rows.
Next row K 2, (K 2 tog) 3 times, K 2. Place
marker threads.
Work 13 rows, placing marker threads at end of
last row.
Work 8 rows more.
Next row K 2, K 3 tog, K 2.
Work 5 rows.
Next row K 1, K 3 tog, K 1.
Work 3 rows.
Last row K 3 tog. Finish off by drawing yarn
through last st.

Head gusset

Using 2 strands A, and 5½mm needles cast on
4 sts for base of nose.
Work in st st, beg with a K row.
Work 8 rows.
9th row K 1, M 1, K to last st, M 1, K 1.
P 1 row.
Rep last 2 rows twice more.
15th row (K 1, M 1) twice, K 2 to last 2 sts,
(M 1, K 1,) twice.
Work 11 rows for top of head.
Dec 1 st at each end of next and every 4th row
until 3 sts rem. Work 3 rows.
Last row K 3 tog, draw end of yarn through last st.

Mane

Using 2 strands of B and 5½mm needles
cast on 33 sts.
1st row K.
2nd row K 1, * Insert right needle into st on left
needle, make loop by putting yarn 3 times

round left needle tip and two fingers of left
hand, draw the loops through the stitch on
right hand needle and slip them back to left
needle, K loops tog as one st, K next st, rep
from * to end.
3rd row K.
4th row K loop as before, * K 1, K 1 loop st, rep
from * to end.
5th row Cast off 18 sts, K to end.
6th row Work loop row as for 2nd row, turn
and cast on 18 sts.
7th row K.
8th row Work as given for 4th row.
9th row K.
10th row Work as for 2nd row.
Cast off.

Ears
Using 2 strands of A cast on 9 sts.
K 6 rows, cast off.
Work second ear in same way.

Tail
Using 2 strands of A, cast on 30 sts.
Work in st st, beg with a K row.
Work 7 rows.
Cast off.

Tail tip
Using 2 strands of B, cast on 9 sts.
Work 6 rows of loop pattern.
Cast off.

To make up
Fold front legs in half and seam along cast on
edges and up leg to cast off edge. Stuff each
section as it is seamed.
Fold back paws in half and seam cast on edges
and cast off edges to form bottom and top of
paw.
Sew cast on edge of body around shaped edge
at start of front gusset. Sew inner edge of back
paws to gusset between first and second
marker threads.
Sew cast off edge of front paws between 3rd
and 4th markers on front gusset. Sew body
between paws to front gusset and sew either
side of top of gusset to body, ending before
cast on sts for face.
Seam face cast on edges together to form lower
jaw and continue seam up to 5th marker.
Pin cast on edge of head gusset over marker for
nose and join either side of head gusset to
either side of face having eleven unshaped

rows at top of head, and final dec at division of sts on back.

Sew ears to each side of head.

Sew mane to top of head bringing separate ends one to either side around below chin.

Fold tail in half and seam. Sew tail tip around one end of tail and sew other end to base of back.

Embroider face.

To work fringe mane

Cut strips of B approx 12.5 cm long.

Take 2 loops, fold in half and draw folded section through knitted stitch. Draw the ends of the yarn through this loop and draw up tight. Work over area to be covered by mane and tail end. Trim when complete.

Chapter 13

Knitting in the round

Knitting in the round has many advantages, particularly for those who dislike sewing garments together once they are completed.

Worked on sets of four or more double-pointed needles, circular knitting is a method of knitting which gives both a perfect shape and reduces the amount of seam sewing, sometimes completely and always to the minimum.

Casting on

The methods given for use with two needles are equally good for round knitting and casting on can be worked in two ways.

1. By casting all the stitches on to one needle and then dividing them evenly onto another two.
2. By casting on one-third of the stitches onto one needle, the second portion onto the second needle and the final third onto the third needle.

Whichever method is used the final edge must look like fig. 96, with the lowest edge completely untwisted. Twisting of stitches is most likely to occur at needle joins so remember to check these carefully.

To begin

Lift the three needles in the left hand and bring the last stitch close to the first stitch. Insert the fourth needle into the first stitch as if to knit and bring the yarn round from the last stitch on the third needle, leaving no slack loop of yarn at the needle join (fig. 97).

Continue to knit along the first needle until all the stitches have been worked. Take the first needle, which is now free of stitches, and work along the second needle; similarly take the second needle when it is free and knit along the third needle. This completes one round.

Other rounds are worked in the same way always using the spare needle to knit the stitches on the following needle.

Fig. 96

Fig. 97

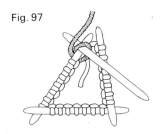

Patterns

The right side of round knitting is always facing the knitter and this makes coloured patterned work much easier to see as there are no awkward wrong side rows to cause confusion. Patterns supplied in chart form link quickly with the work and can be seen at a glance. These charts are now read from right to left on every row.

Stitch differences

One major difference between flat knitting and round knitting is that knitting every round no longer produces garter stitch. To do so it is necessary to work one round knit and one round purl alternately. Knitting every round produces stocking stitch and reversed stocking stitch is obtained by working every round purl. This may sound confusing before starting to work but it becomes second nature as soon as knitting is begun.

Joining yarn

Yarn should still be joined by darning in the ends on side areas and, although there are no seams now, the yarn should be joined at the beginning of a new round.

Marker threads

A coloured marker thread can be placed at the start of a round and carried up as the work progresses to mark side seam and also the start of the round (see page 34).

Shaping

Circular knitting does not mean that work is now only tubular, and increasing and decreasing are carried out in the same way as described for flat knitting.

Avoiding seams

Dresses, sweaters and skirts can now be made without any seams. A sweater can be knitted round to the armholes, divided here and worked in rows to the shoulders which are grafted together. Once the shoulders are joined, the neckline can have a neat rounded edge or a polo collar added and then stitches can be picked up around the armhole and knitted down to the cuff for the sleeve.

Circular needles

For large circular garments circular needles can be a great help. (Fig. 98.) Casting on is worked as for a set of needles and from then on both hands hold the weight of the work evenly which is less tiring than changing it from hand to hand.

Drawback

The only difficulty is that circular needles cannot

Fig. 98

be used for every garment. There must be enough stitches to reach from tip to tip of the needle so they cannot be used for small items such as gloves, socks or baby garments which must be knitted on a set of needles.

Advantage

Their greatest advantage, other than for working sweater bodies and skirts, is that they do not have to be used only for circular work but can be used as a pair of needles by not joining the first and last stitch but by working backwards and forwards in rows instead.

Their length is longer than that of normal needles and means that many things can be tackled with them that had previously to be seamed together. Button bands around both sides of a jacket can be knitted up in one go. Scarves can be knitted lengthwise, which makes a whole host of ideas for stripes and patterns possible.

Jackets, cardigans and coats can all be made seamless to the armholes and skirts can be worked from the waist down for easy hem alterations, or upwards if preferred, but whichever direction is chosen there need be no seams to spoil the hang of the fabric.

Project: Scarf

A circular needle holds far more stitches than can be worked with a pair of needles making it possible to work a scarf lengthwise instead of across the width of the fabric. This alters the appearance of patterns and makes it easy to knit vertical stripes. This scarf is not only striped but uses a lengthened stitch which makes it quick to work.

Materials

The yarn used is Patons Husky.
3×50 g balls of main shade, A.
3×50 g balls of contrast, B.
One $6\frac{1}{2}$ mm circular needle 80 cm long.

continued on page 113

Opposite *Ribbed Jacket (pattern on p. 122). Thick Fisherman's rib makes a warm but light fabric.*
Overleaf *Narrow-striped version and Lace-panelled version of Basic V-necked Sweater (pattern for both versions on p. 93)*

108

Measurements

Approx 25 cm wide and 165 cm long, without fringe.

Tension

Approx 7 sts to 5 cm measured over garter st worked on a $6\frac{1}{2}$ mm needle.
One pattern repeat of 6 rows measures approx 4 cm.

The method

Using $6\frac{1}{2}$ mm needle and A, cast on 250 sts.
1st row Using A, K.
2nd row K.
3rd row K.
4th row K. Leave A hanging at side of work.
5th row Using B, * K 1 putting yarn twice round needle, rep from * to end of row.
6th row Using B, * P next st, dropping extra loop to lengthen st, rep from * to end of row.
Leave B hanging at side edge.
Rep rows 1 to 6, 4 times more or as required, then rows 1 to 4 once.
Cast off.

Knitted fringe

Using $6\frac{1}{2}$ mm needle and B cast on 9 sts.
Knit until strip measures same length as scarf end.
Cast off 3 sts only, then cut end and draw through last st on needle. Allow other stitches to drop off needle and unravel until they become loops instead of stitches.
Sew strip to either end of scarf.
A more dense fringe can be made by working extra strips and sewing on reverse side of end as well as on other side.
Longer loops can be made by casting on additional stitches.

Project: Mittens

Round knitting is often neglected because more than two needles are used. The short double-pointed needles used for this seamless knitting fit easily between the fingers and are no more difficult to use than two needles. Gloves, mittens, caps and socks are far more easily worked in this

---

Opposite *Scarf knitted on circular needles (pattern on p. 108) and mittens (pattern on p. 113)*

way as there is no sewing up once the knitting is completed.

A basic design for mittens may have pattern added by using more than one colour or colours added by embroidery once the mittens are completed.

Materials

The yarn used is Patons Double Knitting Wool.
1 × 50 g ball.
1 set of 4 mm double-pointed needles.

Measurements

To fit an average adult hand.

Tension

11 sts and 15 rounds to 5 cm.

The method

Using 4 mm needles cast on 40 sts and arrange on 3 needles.

Curl the needles round and join the 1st and last sts using the 4th needle.

Work 7.5 cm in K 2, P 2 rib.

Cont in st st (in round knitting this means knit every st of each round).

K 6 rounds.

Shape thumb

1st round K 2, K up thread before next st to M 1, K 1, M 1, K to end.

Place a coloured marker in the st between the made sts to mark the centre of the thumb gusset.

K 1 round.

3rd round K 2, M 1, K 3, M 1, K to end of round.

K 1 round.

Cont in this way inc 1 st at either side of thumb gusset until 5 sts have been inc at either side.

K 1 round.

Next round K 2, sl 11 sts for thumb onto holder, turn work and using two needle method cast on to left needle 7 sts, turn and K to end.

Next round K 1, sl 1, K 1, psso, K 5, K 2 tog, K to end.

K 1 round.

Next round K 1, sl 1, K 1, psso, K 3, K 2 tog, K to end.

Next round K 1, sl 1, K 1, psso, K 1, K 2 tog, K to end.

Cont in st st until work measures 2.5 cm less than required length to finger tips.

Shape top

Dec 5 sts evenly on next round. K 1 round.

Rep last 2 rounds once.

Dec 5 sts evenly on next 5 rounds. Cut yarn

leaving an end to darn through rem loops and
draw up or place sts tog and graft.

Thumb
Rejoin yarn to thumb sts, K 6 sts from holder
onto first needle, K rem 5 sts from holder onto
second needle, and K up 7 sts along 7 cast on
sts.
Work in rounds of st st until 5 cm long or 2
rounds less than required length.
Next round * K 1, K 2 tog, rep from * to end.
Last round * K 2 tog, rep from * to end.
Cut yarn and thread end through rem sts. Draw
up and secure on wrong side.
Make 2nd mitten in same way.

Chapter 14

Finishing touches

The finishing off of a garment, both pressing (if required) and the seaming of knitted sections together, is as important as the knitting itself. A well-knitted garment can be completely spoiled by bad making up in which untidy seams which may be uneven, too loose or dragged too tight if the wrong stitch is used, all detract from the smartness which can be easily obtained.

Blocking

Most pieces of knitting, with the exception of some using man-made fibres, must be blocked and pressed before being made up. Blocking means pinning out the knitted sections to size and shape ready for pressing. A good shape at this stage makes for easy seaming and is worth the time it undoubtedly takes.

Place the sections wrong side up on a padded ironing table or board. Then before pinning and as the pins are placed check to see that all horizontal and vertical lines are horizontal and vertical, that both sides match and are even and that the pieces are their correct measurements (fig. 99), repinning if necessary. The edges must not be dragged out to points by using too few pins or placing them too tightly. Pins are speared through the edge of the knitting at a slight angle and are held in place by the pad they are on beneath the ironing sheet (fig. 100).

Pressing

All knitting should be covered with a clean cotton cloth so that it does not come in direct contact with the iron. Strictly speaking, pressing is not a good term to use as the full weight of the iron should not be placed on the knitting nor should the iron be moved backwards and forwards. The heated iron should be held against the surface of the cloth, whether this is dry or wet and the heat or steam should be allowed to

Fig. 99

Fig. 100

smooth the fibres of the yarn.

When damp pressing make certain that every area is completely dry before removing the pins. Allow to cool before withdrawing the pins and starting to sew the seams.

Avoid pressing areas of ribbing or garter stitch; these should be gently steamed back if they are inadvertently flattened during pressing.

Seaming

The choice of the correct stitch for the type of seam is almost as important as working it evenly and neatly. Seams should be as invisible as possible and not so tight that the knitting is shortened or so loose that they can be pulled apart. They should, if visible, present a smooth line that does not fail to follow the line of stitches whenever possible.

Ribbing and stocking stitch can be joined invisibly by using a seam worked on the right side.

Yarn

Whenever possible seam with the garment yarn. When this is too thick or is not smooth try to divide it. When a yarn is so spun that it will not divide try to purchase a matching shade in a similar type of yarn that is finer. Do not seam wool with man-made fibres or man-made fibres with wool.

An invisible seam

This is a form of vertical grafting with the stitches at either side meeting exactly so that the seam disappears.

Thread a wool needle with yarn and secure to the base of one of the sides to be seamed. For best results work one complete stitch in from the edge. Bring the yarn to the right side and then take it under the first two strands of yarn between the first and second stitch from the edge, bringing it out at the top of the strands (fig. 101). Take it across to the other section and under the first two strands, one stitch in from the edge, bringing it out at the top of the two strands. Draw the yarn up so that the two edges meet and the first stitch on each side is turned in (fig. 102). Repeat this procedure by returning to the first edge and lifting the next two strands and then lifting the corresponding two strands on the second side and drawing the edges firmly together (fig. 103).

Continue in this way until the two edges are joined. The yarn should be drawn tight as the work progresses without dragging the seam so

Fig. 101

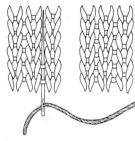

Fig. 102

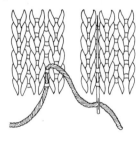

Fig. 103

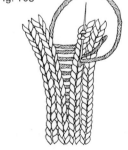

that it is shortened. This method can also be used in reverse working from the top of the seam downwards.

If you are using a chunky yarn, thicker than double knitting, it is advisable to work only one strand at a time.

Ribbing

Ribbed edges should always be sewn up with a woven seam which joins the two edges side by side without leaving stitches showing on the wrong side (fig. 104).

Hold the edges together with the wrong side facing and after securing the end of yarn on one side take it under both strands of one stitch, then across to lift both strands on the other side. This can be worked directly on the edge stitches which are drawn together as the seam is worked.

Shoulder seams

These can be worked by a horizontal grafting which is similar to the invisible seam but is worked across the fabric.

Work on the right side and draw the two edges together by passing the threaded needle under both strands of one stitch then across and under both strands of the first stitch on the other side. Continue by returning to pass under both threads of the next stitch and also both threads of the next stitch on the other side. Work to the end of the shoulder before finishing off the yarn.

Backstitch seams

Backstitch seams are worked in very much the same way as needlework seams but care must be taken to pass between stitches and to work in a line with the stitches wherever possible.

When used on shoulders both loops of the cast off or cast on edges must be left untouched with the seam making as straight a line as possible immediately below (fig. 105). These loops should never be allowed to show on the right side. Backstitch seams are useful wherever an edge is not even as on many lace patterns.

Precaution

Even when matching stitch for stitch, seams should be lightly pinned before working. It is all too easy to finish with one edge longer than the other and pinning will keep this from happening.

Slip stitched hems

Hems which are turned to the wrong side can be slip stitched in place using the garment yarn. Catch a stitch from the edge of the hem and the back of the stitch on the wrong side of the garment behind it, working along the hem (fig.

Fig. 104

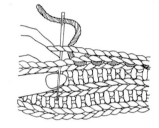

Fig. 105

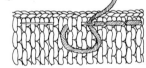

Fig. 106

106). Although the stitches should not be slack do not pull the yarn as tight as for a seam. There should be just enough tension to hold the hem in place against the other side of the work. If the stitch is drawn too tight it will show on the right side of the work and when pressed the hard mark of the cast on or cast off edge will also be visible on the right side of the garment.

Casing stitch

Waist elastic should be held in place around the edge of the garment by working casing stitch closely to cover the elastic circle. Seam the elastic first and hold it inside the waistband immediately below the edge with pins. Using a wool needle and the garment yarn work as shown in the diagram lifting a stitch on the edge, carrying the yarn across the width of the elastic and lifting a stitch from immediately below the elastic (fig. 107). This should not be drawn so tightly that the elastic curls or the casing is pulled round it.

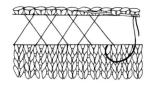

Fig. 107

Zippers

Zippers should be pinned into place on a flat surface, then tacked before attempting to back-stitch on the wrong side (fig. 108). A firmer join will be made if ordinary sewing thread—silk for wool and synthetic for man-made fibres—is used and the zip edges should be backstitched onto the knitting. The extreme edge can then be slip stitched against the wrong side of the knitting so that it does not curl in use.

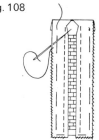

Fig. 108

Grafting

Grafting is a means of joining two edges so that the texture of the stitches is unbroken. It can be worked in two ways either—

1. While the knitting is on the needles, in place of casting off as at the toe of a sock.
2. After the pieces have been cast off, either worked horizontally as on two shoulder edges or vertically on two side edges.

Stocking stitch, reversed stocking stitch and garter stitch can all be joined invisibly by grafting. By using this technique the stitches on one side of the work flow directly into the stitches on the other side without a harsh cast off edge or the firmness that a seam produces.

Grafting stocking stitch

Place the needles, which should hold equal numbers of stitches, one behind the other, with the right side facing the knitter on the front needle and the purl side facing inwards on the back needle. The needle points should be pointing to the right and a length of yarn left at the right. A separate length of yarn can be used if insufficient has been left.

Thread the yarn into a wool needle. Insert it into the first stitch as if to purl and draw the yarn through. * Insert the needle into the first stitch on the back needle as if to purl, draw the yarn through and slip the stitch off the needle. Insert the needle through the next stitch on the back needle as if to knit, draw the yarn through, but leave the stitch on the back needle. Return to the front needle and insert the needle through the first stitch as if to knit, draw the yarn through and slip the stitch off the knitting needle. Insert it into the next stitch on the front needle as if to purl, draw the yarn through but leave the stitch on the needle. Work from the * until all the stitches have been worked off (fig. 109).

Reversed stocking stitch is worked in exactly the same way working on what is the wrong side (i.e. the smooth side) and turning the work out to the other side when complete.

Garter stitch grafting

For garter stitch the needles must be placed so that the smooth side of the last row is placed on the front needle and the ridged side on the back. The stitches are then worked off, as for stocking stitch with two stitches from the front and two from the back needle (fig. 110). On both needles the yarn is passed through the stitch as for the front needle, inserting it as if to purl. When it is drawn through the first stitch is slipped off the knitting needle, the wool needle is inserted into the next stitch as if to knit and the yarn drawn through but the stitch left on the needle.

Horizontal grafting

Horizontal edges that have been completed are grafted by passing the yarn alternately under two threads beneath the cast off edge on one side and under two threads in the same position on the other side until all stitches are drawn together.

An invisible cast on

As a substitute cast on edge this invisible edge gives a rounded, more finished appearance and can be used to replace an edge which is not going to be seamed and which is worked in rib.

Using a contrasting yarn of the same thickness as the yarn to be used for the garment cast on with the two needle method half the required number of stitches.

Fig. 109

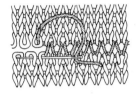

Fig. 110

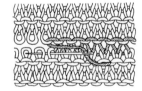

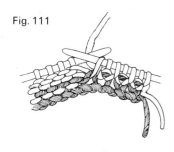

Fig. 111

Change to using the correct yarn and work four rows in stocking stitch beginning with a purl row.

Fold the edge up and on the next row purl the first stitch and lift the first loop that shows on the contrast yarn working it as a knit stitch, purl the next stitch on the needle and knit up the next loop showing on the contrast (fig. 111). Work along all the loops and stitches in this way until the number of loops equals the number of stitches required. Remove the contrast yarn and complete the edge in ribbing. Where the required number is an odd number one stitch can be increased on the first row of rib to give the correct amount.

Picking up dropped stitches

Accidents will happen and the most careful knitter will be faced with picking up stitches which have unintentionally been dropped from the needle.

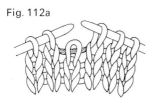

Fig. 112a

Picking up a few stitches can be worked without unravelling any work. Insert a fine needle through any dropped stitches so that they are held in place. Using the correct size for the actual garment insert a needle through the stitch and also under the first strand of yarn above the stitch. Draw the strand back through the loop to form a new loop. Repeat this, gradually working up the ladder of strands until the dropped stitch is up to the level of the stitches still on the needle (fig. 112).

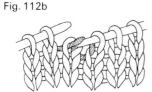

Fig. 112b

Other stitches are picked up in the same way. Before starting to knit again make sure that all the stitches are correct, and should any be twisted, drop them and lift them correctly again.

This method can be used on stocking stitch and also applies to reversed stocking stitch, where the stitch should be picked up on the smooth side of the fabric. Picking up stitches on garter stitch uses the same method but it is necessary to turn the work after each strand is drawn through to retain the ridged appearance of garter stitch.

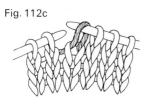

Fig. 112c

Where many stitches have been dropped it is better to slip all the stitches off the needle, gently ease the yarn out of the rows until the level of the lowest stitch has been reached and then slip the loops back onto a needle. Starting from the left take back one more row to be certain that the correct number of stitches has been retained and that the stitches are not twisted or split. To do this insert the left needle into the first stitch on the right needle, draw the yarn tight with the right fingers and let the stitch slip off the right needle tip. Repeat this along the row until all the stitches are on the left needle.

A needle one size smaller can always be used to pick up loops and also for rows which are to be taken back, but remember to change to the correct size when the knitting has been repaired and is ready to be worked again.

Project: Ribbed jacket

Neat pockets and buttonholes give a good finish to a garment. This ribbed jacket, worked in chunky fisherman's rib, uses a clever way of making buttonholes on both front and pockets without knitting them into the fabric.

Materials
The yarn used is Jaeger Spiral spun.
13 (14:15:16) 50 g balls.
1 pair each $3\frac{1}{4}$ and 4 mm needles.
6 buttons.

Measurements
To fit an 80 (85: 90: 95) bust, 32 (34: 36: 38) in.
Length from shoulder: 65 (66: 67: 69) cm.
Sleeve seam: 40 cm, or as required.

Tension
Approx 5 sts and 10 rows to 2.5 cm over rib worked on 4 mm needles unstretched.

Special Abbreviation
K 1 b — K 1 inserting the needle into the space beneath, on the row below, and knitting the stitch in the usual way, see page 100.

Back
Using $3\frac{1}{4}$ mm needles cast on 101 (109: 117: 125) sts.
1st row Sl 1, K to end.
2nd row Sl 1, P 1, * K 1 b, P 1, rep from * to last st, P 1.
Change to 4 mm needles.
Cont in rib patt as set rep 1st and 2nd rows throughout, working until 40 cm from cast on edge, ending with a 2nd row.

Shape raglan
Cast off 2 sts at beg of next 2 rows.
3rd row K 3, K 2 tog tbl, K to last 5 sts, K 2 tog, K 3.
4th row K 3, rib to last 3 sts, K 3.
5th row K.
6th row K 3, rib to last 3 sts, K 3.

Rep rows 3 to 6, 3 times more then 3rd and 4th rows until 35 (37:39:41) sts rem, ending with a 4th row.
Cast off.

Pocket linings
Using 4 mm needles cast on 28 sts.
Work in st st beg with a K row. Work until lining measures 10 cm, ending with a K row.
Leave on holder until required.
Work 2nd lining in same way.

Left front
Using $3\frac{1}{4}$ mm needles cast on 51 (55:59:63) sts.
Work as for Back until 12.5 cm from cast on edge, ending with a 2nd row.
Place pocket
Next row Work 12 (14:16:18) sts, cast off 28 sts, work 11 (13:15:17) sts.
Next row Rib 11 (13:15:17) rib across 28 sts from 1st pocket lining keeping rib correct with front and having knit side facing front of pocket, rib to end.
Cont in patt until front is 10 rows less than Back to raglan shaping, ending with a 2nd row.
Shape front
Inc 1 st at centre front edge on next and every foll 10th row until 8 increases in all have been worked, working extra stitches into rib, AT SAME TIME after working 9 rows more shape raglan as follows —
Cast off 2 sts, K to last st, inc (2nd front inc).
Patt 1 row.
3rd row K 3, K 2 tog tbl, K to end.
4th row Patt to last 3 sts, K 3.
5th row K.
6th row Patt to last 3 sts, K 3.
Rep rows 3 to 6, 5 times more working 3rd and 4th front increases on 3rd row of 2nd repeat and 1st row of 5th repeat.
Rep 3rd and 4th raglan shaping rows, working 4 more front dec as stated then work front edge without shaping until 26 (27:28:29) sts rem.
Work on these sts until strip is long enough to reach to centre back neck allowing 2.5 cm for sleeve top. Cast off.

Right front
Work as for Left front reversing all shaping and pocket position.
Pocket rows will read —

Next row K 11 (13: 15: 17), cast off 28 sts, K to end.

Next row Patt 12 (14: 16: 18), work across 28 sts from 2nd pocket lining, patt to end. Increase stitches are worked 8 times on centre front and raglan shaping is worked by casting off 2 sts at armhole edge when side is same length as Back to armhole.

The raglan decrease is worked thus—

3rd row K to last 5 sts, K 2 tog, K 3.

4th row K 3, rib to end.

5th row K.

6th row K 3, rib to end.

These 4 rows are rep 5 times more and then 3rd and 4th rows are rep as for other side.

Sleeves

Using $3\frac{1}{4}$ mm needles cast on 41 (43: 45: 47) sts.

Rep 1st and 2nd rows as for Back until work measures 7.5 cm, ending with a 2nd row.

Next row P, inc 10 times evenly across row. Change to 4 mm needles.

Cont in rib, beg with a K row to reverse side on which pattern shows, inc 1st at each end of 10th and every foll 10th row until there are 69 (75: 81: 87) sts.

Work without shaping until sleeve measures 40 cm or required length ending with a 2nd row.

Shape raglan

Cast off 2 sts at beg of next 2 rows.

3rd row K 3, K 2 tog tbl, K to last 5 sts K 2 tog, K 3.

4th row K 3, patt to last 3 sts, K 3.

5th row K.

6th row K 3, patt to last 3 sts, K 3.

Rep rows 3 to 6 twice more, then 3rd and 4th rows until 8 sts rem. Work 1 row.

Cast off.

To make up

Join raglan seams. Sew collar to sleeve tops and back neck, joining collar seam.

Join side and sleeve seams. Slip stitch pocket lining in place.

Border

Using $3\frac{1}{4}$ mm needles cast on 6 sts.

1st row Sl 1, K to end.

Rep 1st row until strip is long enough to reach from cast on edge of left front round collar edge to cast on right front edge. Stitch left front in place before casting off and mark positions for buttons.

Complete knitting strip, stitching into place as sufficient length is worked and leaving gaps for buttons as markers are reached.

Pocket tops

Using $3\frac{1}{4}$ mm needles cast on 6 sts.

Work strip as for button strip to edge each cast off pocket edge.

Sew to pocket leaving central gap for button.

Sew on buttons to correspond with buttonholes.

Index

Needle conversion chart

Metric needle sizes	Old English equivalent
$7\frac{1}{2}$ mm	No 1
7 mm	No 2
$6\frac{1}{2}$ mm	No 3
6 mm	No 4
$5\frac{1}{2}$ mm	No 5
5 mm	No 6
$4\frac{1}{2}$ mm	No 7
4 mm	No 8
$3\frac{1}{2}$ mm	No 9
$3\frac{1}{4}$ mm	No 10
3 mm	No 11
$2\frac{1}{2}$ mm	No 12
$2\frac{1}{4}$ mm	No 13
2 mm	No 14